Is There Anybody There?

To Marylin
love light and laughter
Bryan.
2020

Bryan Gibson

Is There Anybody There?

by

Bryan Gibson

Regency Press (London & New York) Ltd.
Chaucer House, Chaucer Business Park,
Kemsing, Sevenoaks, Kent TN15 6PW

Copyright © 1998 by Bryan Gibson
First Published 1998

This book is copyrighted under the Berne Convention. No portion may be reproduced by any process without the copyright holder's written permission except for the purposes of reviewing or criticism, as permitted under the Copyright Act of 1956.

ISBN 0 7212 0971 8

Printed and bound in Great Britain by
Buckland Press Ltd., Dover, Kent.

This book is dedicated to all those
here on the earth plane.
Thanks for the help and support of
the families of those mentioned
in the book.
My very special thanks to
"RUNNING FOOT",
my spirit family and friends
without whose knowledge and guidance
this book could not have been written.
Thanks too, to Monica Underwood and
John Brett for the help, support,
patience, and understanding which
has helped me complete this book.

Bryan

CONTENTS

For Val, a dedication	11
Poem – My Friend Works As A Medium	14
Introduction	15
Chapter One Running Foot's Sense of Humour	23
Chapter Two Gossiping With Spirit	25
Chapter Three Laughing During Demonstrations	27
Chapter Four Short But Funny Stories	30
Poem – I'm Very Well Thank You	38
Chapter Five Within The Hour	39
Chapter Six The Lady Of The House	40
Chapter Seven The Spirit World	44
Chapter Eight The Knocks And Doubts	47
Chapter Nine Obstacles	49
Chapter Ten Sometimes, It Is So Hard To Be A Medium	53
Chapter Eleven Claire And Lindsey	55
Chapter Twelve Jane And Carl	58
Chapter Thirteen Andrew	62
Poem – A Brother's Love	65
Chapter Fourteen Richard (Rich)	66
Chapter Fifteen Steve (Sket)	70
Messages From The Grave	75
Chapter Sixteen Paul	76
Poem – A Tribute To Paul	79
Chapter Seventeen A Tribute To Vi	80
Chapter Eighteen Demonstrations	83
Chapter Nineteen Communication From Spirit	87
Chapter Twenty Different People – Different Lives	90
Happy Medium	96

Chapter Twenty-One Marilyn	97
Chapter Twenty-Two Messages About The Future	99
Chapter Twenty-Three Help From Spirit	102
Chapter Twenty-Four Should I?	104
Chapter Twenty-Five Linking With The Law	106
Spirit Led Me	109
Chapter Twenty-Six Missing	111
Chapter Twenty-Seven Problems Yet To Be Solved	114
Chapter Twenty-Eight Where To Now?	117
Chapter Twenty-Nine Germany	119
Chapter Thirty "Century Radio"	122
Chapter Thirty-One The Sitting	126
Chapter Thirty-Two For Poppy	130
Poem – Tribute To Poppy	132
Poems	133
The Medium	134
Seasons Of Life	135
My Son	136
Look Forward To The Future	137
Mother, Oh Mother	138
Did I Imagine?	139
Acknowledgements	141
Books by Bryan Gibson	143

LIST OF ILLUSTRATIONS

Bryan Gibson	Frontispiece
The author at Belfast S.N.U. Spiritualist Church	12
Val	12
Val's father	12
Mount Lane Farm	40
Mrs Mastin (Grace)	41
Claire and Lindsey	56
Letter from Carl's mother	59
Carl Warriner and his son	60
Andrew	63
Poem from Sket's daughter, Michelle	73
Paul	74
Steve (Sket)	74
Richard	74
Vi and her parrot	81
Demonstration at Woolsthorpe	84
Demonstrating with Coral Polge	85
Sam Tomlinson	93
Relaxing at home with friends	100
Germany, 1997	120
Poppy	130

FOR VAL

I should like to dedicate this book to Val, my cousin who passed to spirit on 17th September 1997, aged 51.
   It is good to realise that Val will now be reunited with her father, my Uncle Fred, who left for spirit in 1970. Unfortunately, this meant that he missed out on most of the special moments which a father usually can enjoy in watching his family growing up around him. Val was, in fact, the eldest of the family but the youngest – Andrew – was born around the time of his passing and therefore did not have the chance to know his father.
   Because both my mother and father and also Val's mother and father were brothers and sisters, as cousins. I suppose we were closer than most and we were very much alike. At one time in my early teens I lived with Uncle Freddy and Aunty Bet for a short time. I was then working in Woolworth's in Newark prior to starting my nursing career and afterwards Val and her sister, Beryl, stayed in touch and visited me in London.
   On returning to Lincolnshire in 1984, I became much closer to Val and her family. When I developed my spiritual gift it was a lovely surprise to find that Val took an interest even though, to begin with, she didn't understand it. Nonetheless, she – together with her husband, Mike, and daughter, Joanne, her brother David and her sister Beryl – would frequently come to support me whenever I was giving a demonstration of mediumship locally.
   During the course of 1996, Val was suddenly taken ill and developed what the doctors first took to be diabetes but shortly discovered was cancer of the pancreas. During this period, Val spent many periods in hospital but never gave up fighting. Her daughter, Joanne, had married and was by then expecting Val's first grandchild, which encouraged her to fight on a determination which was very obvious when little Sophie was born and the baby's arrival seemed to give her fresh strength.
   The next goal which mattered to her a great deal was to see her son, Ian, marry in 1998 but, sadly she did not manage to achieve that, nor to see, Matthew, her youngest son settle into his new life either.
   Just prior to leaving for my visit to Belfast. I visited Val and we were able to spend time together. She wanted to know all about my work over there and, although she was showing signs of deterioration her spirit was still strong.

Serving at Belfast S.N.U. Spiritualist Church, September 1997, with the candle lit in memory of Val.

My cousin, Val, with her granddaughter, Sophie.

Val's father, my uncle, Freddie.

I did not realise that this would be the last time I should see her although she was due to go into the local Hospice for the family to have a much needed rest for a while.

Early in the morning of 17th September 1997, the telephone rang in the flat where I was staying in Belfast and I was informed that Val has passed into spirit. I knew that Val would want me to continue with my work there rather than return home and so I decided to stay as arranged and return home in time for her funeral which was to be the following Tuesday.

The service was beautiful, not religiously solemn, as that was not Val's way, but with modern music by Robson & Jerome and with one special hymn, "Make me a channel of your peace" another favourite of Val's. As Val was taken from the church she left to Elton John's "Candle in the Wind"; it was all very peaceful and beautiful.

Since Val has been in the world of spirit, I have often experienced her presence with me during demonstrations and I was very aware of her recently when I was in North Wales with psychic artist, John Brett, doing a demonstration to raise money for a young man named Edward who was suffering from cancer. Just before the event began, the tape being played was, "Make me a channel of your peace" and I have never felt a surge of energy such as Val gave me that night.

Now, I often say (just before I begin a demonstration), "Come on Val. Let's show them what spirit is all about!" and the evidence and the laughter flows freely.

You can therefore understand why, on this occasion, I particularly wish to make this my special tribute to Val. Uncle Freddy, Uncle Roy. Uncle George and all my many family members who am now happy and peaceful in the wonderful word of Spirit.

My friend works as a medium

My friend works as a medium,
"A medium what?", you say.
I'll tell you what he's good at
Although it may take all day.

First of all, he listens –
To them, and you, just so
The things he hears can be passed on
For all who need to know.

It isn't so much that his hearing is good
Or his eyes see farther than most,
Nor is it a matter of trying to prove
He's well qualified for the post.

The thing is he talks to spirits
Who get him to do jobs as brave
As saying they're just as alive as us
In a land beyond the grave.

He supports what he says with evidence
That makes the agnostic flinch,
Quoting names and dates and numbers
Or addresses at a pinch.

He has no way of knowing
Whether data he gives is right
Apart from responsive faces
Filled with joy and hope and light.

He works with love and laughter
For a very important Boss
And if he was made redundant,
We'd suffer enormous loss.

So I'm glad my friend's a medium,
That we all can live within range
Of someone like him who operates
Spirit's telephone exchange.

MONICA UNDERWOOD

INTRODUCTION

There is so much beauty around us all which we seldom see. The unseen world which surrounds us all is full of spiritual energy and overflowing with wonder.

When we turn our attention for a moment away from this physical world of ours and focus on other levels of knowing and feeling, we find enough exciting surprises to keep us all happy for ever.

The stories in this book describe some of those joyous moments when people like you and me made the great discovery that life and love are for ever – that there is no death – and that, when the physical body disintegrates, the person who was temporarily using that body detaches from it and moves out, to go adventuring and exploring the other dimensions which are open to us all.

Many of you have told me that you wished you could have read the early books-which I wrote about the people I met through my mediumship, as well as the more recent ones. For you, I have rewritten the original stories and hope you will enjoy them; this book includes them as well as all the new material which has not been published before. This book is especially for you.

The stories are endless because the pathway we tread is endless; we keep moving on nearer and nearer the goal – until we find that the goal is really the place we started out from – and that is a place filled with perfect Love and Light, and that each of us is connected to it all.

I hope that these earlier stories will bring you as much pleasure as they did to me, as I remembered each one. For me, it was like meeting an old friend from whom I had been out of touch for a while as I came to each one afresh. It was like I had been talking to them yesterday but then, Love is like that. The lovely moments are like pearls strung on a cord of love; they are all connected and there really is no separation. As the stories, both old and new, in this book will show you, truly there never is.

When our most treasured companions and friends leave us, it is a shock. Our family, friends and pets can be here one minute and gone the next and we feel terribly alone. We are not. Although we cannot see or hear them, they are really very close, and those who have loved us love us still.

We all find this very difficult to handle and the fear, frustration and anger we experience are a natural part of the grieving process. We can feel anger towards them for leaving us – sometimes when life has only just begun; sometimes we feel that our only wish is to join them or that we had gone instead, but, my friend, they are still with you. Their presence is all around you and, through their spirit energy they continue to enable you to carry on, keeping their memory alive and encouraging you to achieve all the things that you had planned to do, things you talked about whilst they were here on earth. They wish to give you the strength to bring up the children in the ways that had been intended before their sudden departure, to make the moves which were already being put into motion. These things are part of what your loved ones are trying to help you to do.

I know that it is easy for those of us lucky enough to be gifted at communicating with people in the world of spirit to say such things when you who have been left behind want to know why you do not see, feel or hear your loved ones as we do. In some cases it is possible for you to do the same, but it is difficult for spirit to reach you when you are surrounded by tension and painful emotion.

Many people try to explain away the unexpected moments of awareness, but you may be lucky enough to experience the feeling of a loved one's presence, the smell of their perfume or tobacco around you.

This is an easy way for spirit to make you aware of your loved Ones presence and, although many people dismiss such things as a coincidence or find a down-to-earth reason to explain them away, they frequently happen particularly at times when you feel most in need of support and reassurance or perhaps when you have been talking with friends or family about those who have gone.

At such times, spirit energy may be communicated to you through a memory of the loved one, a scent, a tobacco smell, or the very strong aroma of a particular flower of which they were fond. As you do, they too send out their thoughts and try to make you aware of their presence around you, giving you comfort and encouragement, attempting to bring you the assurance that all will be well and that they are thinking of you.

I sincerely hope that, through my own experiences in spiritual communication, it will be possible to unlock a few of the myths and unanswered questions which we are afraid to ask in case others find us foolish or strange.

Each one of us has the ability to communicate with Spirit, but the ways in which we do so vary. We can do so directly or through others who may also have suffered loss themselves and understand our feelings. Spiritual healing at such times can also be a very real help. When we have lost someone who is very dear to us, it can be difficult to believe the evidence of our eyes and ears in the event of our seeing or hearing them and the question of whether we have imagined it is uppermost in our minds.

Sometimes this may be the case, but often they really do manage to provide us with a brief glimpse of them or the sound of their voice perhaps calling our name. It's meant to reassure us that they are still with us, at peace, and only just that touch away.

At times when our minds are switched off from material problems and worries, such as when we are drifting off to sleep or about to awake, with our physical energies relaxed, we are much more receptive to links with the spirit world. Having talked to many people who have had similar experiences, a pattern emerges in which visual or audible communication seems to occur mostly when we are at our most relaxed as then our loved ones are more able to overcome the barriers we create in our normal, waking state. Obviously, we all ask, "Is it my imagination?", but it is at such times that our earth body and our spiritual body can unite and allow communication and messages from our loved ones to be received.

During my many sittings with people from many different walks of life, I find that a very special connection is made. Not only the people who have come to visit in the hope of receiving word of their dear ones, but I also have been included in the great feeling of union. I can only describe such times as unbelievable experiences where the wonderful communication is so positive and real that I know there is no division between the communicator and myself. For the brief duration of the sitting, I am myself able to feel the great emotion and power transmitted by that person and such experiences only cause me to strive for ever greater levels of communication with spirit which, with patience and more learning, I know I can achieve. I have no fear of my gift, its strength, or the responsibility it brings for to me it is utterly natural and the way it was meant to be. Communicators do not control my life because spirit and I work together as a family and, by taking this attitude, I know that my gift will be used only for right reasons, bringing help to those who come seeking spiritual communication and guidance to enable them to walk the right pathway for their lives, whatever the nature of their problems.

When working with my gift, help often comes to the sitter via a friend or a member of the family who knows them well and wishes to help. Sometimes the messages may be relayed from a grandparent who perhaps passed into the world of spirit before the questioner was even born, but that grandparent may well have followed the progress of the young person through childhood and into adult life and is as willing to offer love and help as any grandparent on the earth plane. The message may be presented emotionally or unemotionally, with natural, logical advice which they know the person will understand, recognising their freedom of choice to accept or reject the spiritual guidance offered and to make their own decisions as they feel they are right for them. No-one from spirit should come down and say, "You must do what we say"; they try to offer what they know is good advice for you but it is entirely up to each and everyone of us choose which pathway it is right for us to follow.

My own experiences are very different one from another in the sittings which take place. People come to see me for very different reasons and the response from spirit varies according to the needs of the sitter.

If you are lucky enough to have a strong, positive spirit person wishing to communicate with you, what usually happens is that he or she will open up the sitting with a strong link between you and them, such as the month of their birthday or passing into spirit, or perhaps an anniversary. This is usually followed by information on the way in which they left the earth plane, stating perhaps illnesses they suffered or giving details of any accident which occurred and, if the link is good enough, giving their name and relationship to the sitter. Until they are able to provide definite evidence of who they are, the communication may seem a little vague. Although most people will accept the name of "Mum", "Dad", "Grandma" or "Grandad", I feel it is much more important to be able to give their name as well. To the receiver of the message it is extra confirmation that it is indeed coming from their loved one and also lets them be sure that it is not a case of them trying to make the message fit what they want to believe.

In many sittings, filled with the thoughts of the spirit person and details of their life, although everything fits into place, it will not be until the end of the communication that they give their name. These people do not change when they leave the earth plane and their personality remains as it was when they were here. The physical body is left behind, but their spirit and personality continue and I believe it is much more important to be able to convey this and to get this across even than their name, in order to provide evidence which can be recognised.

I know from experience that some spirit communicators can easily cause problems within group sittings. If they appeared to be easy-going and pleasant when the person on the earth plane had been difficult and grumpy, their loved ones enquiring after them would never recognise them anyway. It is no good my standing up and saying, "I have with me a very nice gentleman who, when on earth, was always quiet and smiling" if he had been just the opposite. It can also be very difficult not to use the language of the communicator where that was perhaps coarse or particularly "colourful". I can assure you it is sometimes very hard not to let words slip through. It has happened before to me and I am sure it will happen again. The spirit person's recipient in an audience will accept the message, but unfortunately it often offends people who feel such natural messages should be restricted. To me, it is part of an everyday occurrence. Of course, I would never deliberately give off an offensive word, but certain phrases are now part of our everyday language and I feel should be accepted as true communication.

To me, my ability to faithfully pass on the messages of my spirit communicator, is very important and that gift should not be restricted. I feel that this attitude is a problem for many natural mediums who decide not to work in churches for this reason. The gift of mediumship is to enable people in the spirit world to communicate with people on the earth plane and it is important that we, as mediums, do the job to the best of our ability.

The strength of the gift varies from medium to medium. All use their bodies as transmitters of spirit energy to earth, some as clairvoyants, or clairaudients and some as healers. Our strength is according to the work spirit has chosen for us to do and should not be a source of division where we fear each others' various abilities, lest we ourselves should be found wanting.

We can only be as good as our gift and it is up to us to work in the way we believe is right for us personally, either full-time or occasionally – hopefully according to spirit's needs. What is involved here is a natural flow of energy which should be encouraged to flow freely without restriction from others.

It is sad when people try to hold others back. Whatever the age of the spiritually aware person, they should be allowed to communicate what they have to offer. Naturally, the more mature the medium, the more life experience they may be able to incorporate in the understanding they bring to a reading. Our work is not just about giving messages from either guides or spirit communicators. Sometimes it is the combination of our own experience of life with what is relayed from the communicator which can bring depth to a reading, and this knowledge is stored to be drawn upon whenever required, and used to help and comfort those who have need of it.

However, not everyone sees mediums in such a good light as you will see from the following stories.

Nonetheless, I hope that, as you read about the work done by my "spiritual family" and me, you will find yourself not only shedding a tear with us sometimes but also laughing – sometimes gently at us – but mainly with us, as we seek to demonstrate that in absolute truth, there is indeed always somebody there. Mediums are the butt of all sorts of jokes. How often we hear people "taking the mickey" out of clairvoyants and the ways in which they work? To people who think this world is the only reality, it is hardly surprising if they find it hilarious to watch us looking at people they cannot see and talking to people whom they cannot hear. In their shoes, I'd find it all pretty amusing too.

Although the media appear to be somewhat more broad minded these days, we have all seen classic seance scenes on T.V. in which an apparently deranged medium sits surrounded by a circle of fearfully intent old people, eyes half-closed in guttering candlelight, holding each others' hands, awaiting meaningful knocks to indicate answers to their questions, while the medium with eyes raised heavenward calls loudly "Is there anybody there?"

Even today, many people believe this is the only way open for them to communicate with those they love in spirit, and I have known folk be disappointed when coming to visit me, when they find nothing weird happening. Such attitudes deter many from approaching a medium to communicate with those they have lost which is sad, as they miss out on what could well be a beautiful, awakening experience spiritually, and one which can bring love, guidance and peace to each and every one of us.

I should like to reassure all those in doubt that there is absolutely nothing to be afraid of in consulting a medium. Nor are we disturbing the dead, because there is no such thing as death, so how can we disturb them!

As a working medium, I have often had the experience of finding sitters coming to visit me for a communication with their loved ones expressing surprise that I am just an ordinary person like themselves rather than someone who wears strange clothes or sporting a weird hair-do.

They find a warm, well-lit room with no crosses on the wall or crystal balls on the table, no drawn curtains or flickering candles and we do not sit around the table touching hands; everything is as natural as sitting in their own front room having a relaxed, natural conversation with their loved ones, relating happy memories with love and laughter. It is good to be able to laugh at ourselves and to see the humour in other people's view of us, such as in the recent television commercial in which a circle of sitters surround the central crystal ball whilst the medium asks, as ever, "Is there anybody there?" to be answered by an empty crisp packet floating down on to the table from the ceiling! Well, there is certainly somebody there . . . but it is a pity that so many people seriously believe that communication with spirit is remotely similar to any such a setting. How wrong they are?

Laughter, however, is an important part of our work. Not only does it relax people to be able to laugh with the medium – perhaps particularly when he is "taking the mickey" out of himself – but it also enables those in spirit to communicate their own particular sense of humour which they exhibited when on the earth-plane. Frequently we are told of their being around us and seeing something which went amusingly wrong, or seeing us play a joke on someone to have it speedily returned, still smiling at the funny things we do and enjoying laughing with us.

Mind you, for a medium to ask of friends in spirit, "Is there anybody there?" is not as daft as it sounds. It must be every medium's nightmare to stand up on a platform in front of scores of expectant faces awaiting messages from friends and loved ones in spirit, only to discover that no-one wants to communicate and that there is absolutely nothing being said. I know this has happened to some people, and I am always aware that it is possible, as mediums, we should never be over-confident or complacent with our gift or take it for granted. My own feeling is that, where people genuinely seek communication with their loved ones through me, spirit always try to connect and respond. I do not believe spirit let us down, but sometimes we do let them down. We are no different from anyone else, experiencing off-days when ill or having personal problems in our life. Such things create interference in our communication system, creating blurred reception like a T.V. or radio when barriers block the connection between us and spirit. Rather than blaming the sitter or the communicator in spirit, I do try nowadays to run a check on myself, scanning my attitude at the time, how I felt towards the sitter, whether my mind was on any personal problems or whether I was slightly under-par healthwise or going down with a cold. There is learning in every situation and I feel that if we, as mediums, take time to analyse such things, rather than disregarding them as if they do not matter, such difficulties can help us increase our ability rather than acting as stumbling blocks either to the sitters or ourselves. With such attention, sitters would less often go home wondering whether poor communication was their fault or whether the medium was "just rubbish". Our guides can help us improve our understanding and performance; everything in life needs working at, even communicating with spirit.

We are all different, having different gifts and differing abilities, some mediums finding their particular niche in demonstrating to an audience, giving out powerful and convincing evidence in such situations, whereas others may be much more effective when working in a one-to-one setting. We are all aiming for the highest and best we can individually manage and can only achieve whatever is possible for us at the time. I am lucky in being able to work with spirit on a full-time basis, but the many mediums and spiritual workers who cannot do so, and work part-time are just as important to the harmonious spreading of understanding spiritual communication as those of us who do not also have the responsibility for running homes, bringing up families and doing other part-time jobs. Many mediums who are in full time 9-5 jobs or who are self-employed, still find time to work for spirit, using their limited time to develop strong spiritual gifts and serving local churches through their ability to communicate with those in spirit.

The patterns of our lives change through the years and I am sure there must be many mediums who have experienced great frustration during such times of limitation, wanting to commit themselves as totally as possible to working within a spiritual environment. However, material life experience is very necessary and useful. By acquiring a wide experience of material situations, our spiritual understanding of other people's lives is deepened and develops in us an unconditional love for other people and a non-judgmental acceptance of whatever lessons life's pathway has been teaching them.

From my own experiences in life, I now know that suffering, work, emotional problems and coping with other people, as well as all the ups and down of life have improved my sensitivity and awareness and developed my strength and positivity as a medium.

As we progress from childhood to becoming adult, we tread many pathways. The thoughts, ideas and understanding this provides for us develop our discrimination and wisdom. If, like me, you have been fortunate to live a lifetime which has stretched your emotions, required you to make difficult decisions and develop an understanding of people and life itself, you will know that you are now a much stronger person than at the beginning. Such things are all beneficial to our work and communication with spirit. Even a wide range of work experience strengthens us and, when we have a link with a spirit communicator who talks about their work on the earth-plane, a medium who has been in a similar situation will have a deeper understanding of the message more quickly than one who does not, and can build a positive link with the sitter who is meant to receive the message, enabling them easily to accept such a fluent communication from spirit.

As the world of spirit seems to communicate with those of us on the earth-plane, we can offer our life experiences as a means of helping create a link which is capable of reaching the great numbers of people searching for knowledge and proof of spiritual survival. Mediumship is a two-way link. It is not a case of "Stand up, open your mouth and expect spirit to appear". In your experience of human life on earth and our friends' experience of life in spirit, the two worlds unite. That's when that remarkable question, "Is there anybody there?" really becomes meaningful.

The communication can help both levels. Where two people have been separated physically by death, the one left on earth can be comforted and reassured by knowing that the loved one in spirit is still alive and that the bond between them can be just as great as ever, and the one communicating from the spirit world can be overjoyed to have the chance to show he knows what is going on here as well as in his new environment. The medium will have done his job well, happy to know he has been a channel for the two worlds to unite in love, peace and harmony.

Chapter One

RUNNING FOOT'S SENSE OF HUMOUR

Most of you will know of my very special relationship with Running Foot. However, like most mediums, a number of spirit guides work with me – I call them my "spiritual family" and we are very close. They are not always serious; they too have a sense of humour!

Often, I have been given the pleasure of gaining an insight into the earth-life of Running Foot when he was here and am quite used to hearing his very deep, loud laughter, but a recent occurrence really amused me.

Lying, totally absorbed in my own little world, surrounded by the warm comfort of my bath water, I suddenly became aware of the presence of Running Foot and how I looked to him. He placed his head-dress on my head which slowly absorbed the water into the feathers. It drooped heavily and I submerged under the water to much laughter from Running Foot who obviously had decided to teach me that he can play jokes as well as be deeply serious.

Frequently, when I have had a bath since, I've expected him to repeat the performance, but now he just starts singing. His songs are always happy and tell a story. I think he's decided that it's the only way he'll ever be able to get me to stay still long enough to teach me his culture or understand him as a person, as normally for us it is always "all work and no play".

Another startling moment was when I was feeling very bored on a drive to London. The occupants of the cars driving alongside must have thought I was totally mad, as I looked into my driving mirror and burst out laughing. Sitting in the back seat of the car, in full feather, was Running Foot with Sister Catherine – my French nun who helps me – as well as Tommy, the Gurkha soldier and several others, all behaving like children, pulling faces and making a racket. It certainly did the trick, my boredom changed into happy relaxation and, before I knew it, I reached my destination.

On arrival, I told this story to my friends who politely tried to understand. It is lovely when these special people in spirit can come and cheer us up, showing that they still retain the humour they had when here on the material plane. I enjoyed it immensely.

I should have liked to be a fly on the wall after my visit to those particular London friends came to an end. I can't imagine why they have never invited me back since!

Chapter Two

GOSSIPING WITH SPIRIT

Spirit are around us all the time. Their world interpenetrates this one and, from time to time, they take a peek at what we are doing with ourselves – without prying – and tell us about what they have noticed whenever they get a chance to communicate through a medium such as me.

Life may be a very serious business some times, but even we have our laughs – and they certainly do.

Take, for instance, the demonstrations which take place in public. Many are held in local churches, some in theatres, and many in places such as village halls where various organisations put on an evening of clairvoyance to raise money for their particular charity. On such occasions, members of public attend who would not do so otherwise, many of them nervous and not at all sure what to expect or whether they should feel guilty about being there at all. There is so much muddled thinking about the whole subject of psychic awareness and clairvoyance and mediumship gets a very bad press, even though a very large proportion of the population themselves believe at least partially in its claims.

In such circumstances, I am always pleased when spirit come through with natural humour and laughter, enabling those present to relax and realise that their loved ones are just the same as they ever were. They haven't grown horns and a tail just by moving out of their physical bodies; they are the same people, loving or grumpy as ever, able to demonstrate to us their particular interests and idiosyncrasies, so that we have no doubt whatever that the communication is genuine. Once people realise that it is meant to be a two-way conversation and they are expected to answer back, confirming the medium has understood and conveyed the message clearly, they can enjoy the contact with people in spirit who are special to them. Communicators often identify themselves by giving details of their relationship to us, personal information about themself, perhaps what they did in their working life when they were here, or maybe how they passed into the world of spirit. They also use dates of birthdays, anniversaries and events which hold special meaning to us to let us know that what is being said is really coming from someone who knows us personally, and that it is not a case of the medium "making it all up" to impress us.

When the communicator has really established his identity and been accepted by the sitter, it is fun for me to be involved in the gossip which follows. It is so like friends on earth meeting over a cup of tea or coffee, and chatting happily over recent things which have been taking place. People are often surprised when spirit come through with really up-to-date information, talking in detail about things which have happened since they have been gone, such as house moves, new babies which have been born since they left, and the colour of the new carpet in the family sitting room!

Obviously, a medium's job is not always an easy one! Communicators are not always full of sweetness and light – and do not always see eye to eye with those on earth about what is going on here. I try to avoid offending people in my audience, but it is not always easy to deliver messages fluently at the same time as omitting rude comments about someone's new hairdo, and making sure I edit out the swear words which are part and parcel of the way in which the person always spoke when here on earth.

Laughter breaks down many barriers and spirit understand this and love to bring fun and humour into the messages they bring us.

What we are doing is communicating with real people, not just a pale reflection of the person they once were when here on earth. They still have just as much "oomph" as they ever had – they just have more freedom in expressing it. They enjoy it, and so can we.

Many times in public demonstrations, spirit communicators have commented on the family holiday which is coming up and said they are going too, but that they haven't got to pay for it.

Basically, they just want to reassure us that they still exist, that they are still the person we knew and loved (or had difficulty with, as the case may be) and that love and laughter are still just as much part of their life in spirit as they were here on the earth in their physical bodies.

Their new bodies are capable of going where they want, when they want, as they want – unlike ours – but, although the limitations on them have changed so much in their lovely, new world, their personalities are still totally recognisable to us, and what is more, when we join them in the world of spirit, we do not need to fear that we shall not know them. We certainly shall – and they will be waiting for us with love and gentle laughter to show us the ropes in our new environment. The point of a medium's work is to remove fear and fill the space with love.

Our spirit friends work with gentle humour to make sure that is just what happens.

Chapter Three

LAUGHTER DURING DEMONSTRATIONS

Surprise can be the order of the day. Because of the numerous demonstrations I give, there are many stories to relate, but I should like to share with you some of the many amusing situations which have arisen during church and theatre demonstrations as well as group sittings. We all interpret messages according to our particular perception, coloured by our sense of humour, and when working with spirit nothing is predictable and the unexpected can surprise even the medium.

About two years ago, I was asked to give a talk to a group of people belonging to the British Legion. This came about through my landlord, Tom Ransome, who invites these people every February to his home and provides a different speaker for them each year. This time, I was invited – looking forward to the lovely buffet meal which I knew followed the talk – and hoping not to disappoint the visitors, as I was sure that few of them had any idea about mediums or the way in which we work.

On arrival. I found Laythorpe Lodge overflowing with about thirty women and one or two supporting husbands.

Following my introduction to them by Tom, I explained what a medium is and outlined what they might expect from the evening, stating that I would try to unite them with their loved ones in spirit, and asking them to respond clearly to me, creating a nice, enjoyable time together. My first communication was with a lady who was eager to accept a message and who was not afraid to talk to me. Her husband was in spirit, and he came through, giving evidence of how he left for the spirit world. He provided months which related to birthdays and anniversaries and even gave his name to prove his identity. Throughout all this time, whilst the lady readily accepted all her husband's messages, she expressed no emotion whatsoever – As the messages continued, I became aware of a lovely, black labrador dog sitting beside her. The expressions on the faces of the other people present were a picture as, when I gave the lady the information about the dog, she promptly burst into floods of tears and was "over the moon" that the dog had come through. She continued by enthusing about the dog and about how much she missed it, and afterwards – during the delicious meal which Tom had provided – it was noticeable how many people commented on the apparent relative importance to the lady of her husband and her dog:

When we look at life, as individuals our priorities differ considerably. At least the lady was happy. It was obvious that this lovely Labrador brought her much love and pleasure during its life and was still an important aspect of her life, even if she did appear to miss it more than her husband!

When working with spirit, I try always to relay the messages from a communicator in such a way that their family and friends recognise them clearly and know that what is said could not possibly come from anyone but them.

There is a lovely spiritual group in Hopton, Norfolk called "The Guiding Light Church" which I love to visit. Jill and Dave, who run it, and their tireless supporting group are so eager to make every occasion a pleasure, that I always enjoy serving them. Mediums and congregation are made to feel special and are always greeted with a very cheery handshake or a hug even in the midst of setting up the hall, putting out the chairs or setting up the charity stall. Over the period in which I have served this church, there have been a number of occasions which have included memorable emotional and funny experiences, but one stands out with pride of place in my memory.

On that particular occasion, the hall was very full and there was a great deal of love and spiritual power filling the place. Following prayer, hymn-singing and a reading, it was my turn to give the demonstration which moved along happily with messages of love and pleasant memories from those in spirit.

I was then drawn to a lady sitting right at the back of the hall. I told her that I had with me her mother and father who had left the earth-plane for spirit many years ago. They provided details of their passing and personal messages which she accepted. (It was later confirmed to me that this was the first time they had communicated since their passing 26 years before.)

As their communication continued, these two special people talked to their daughter and grand-daughter who was also present, of the changes in the family over the years, where people were living and the work they were involved in. Suddenly, I was aware of a change in the atmosphere and of a lot of laughter. The mother in spirit said to me, "Mention the Ann Summers Party". On asking the two ladies whether they had recently attended a party such as an Ann Summers party, they both collapsed in laughter – and so did many others in the congregation. The mother in spirit said she had been with them that night and laughed about some items on show and the fun people had had trying things on. By then, the imagination of the congregation was working overtime and the whole room was filled with laughter.

Sometimes, it can be very difficult relating such messages at a public meeting in case people are offended, but spirit knew that on this occasion everyone would enjoy the fun, which was a very good thing because the next message was quite specific.

After a pause, the mother said, "Tell my daughter I know about the 'willy-warmer'". The ladies roared with laughter and eventually managed to answer me to say my communicator was correct. Her daughter's husband was a bit prudish and she had ordered one for him for Christmas as a joke. The hall was filled with laughter as spirit had intended, knowing that it would not cause offence there. The ladies' message was accepted with the love and fun which the mother in spirit had shared. It certainly was the highlight of the evening and people were still laughing about it as they left the hall later. Once again, spirit had shown that there is nothing like laughter to make us forget our worries and troubles for a while. Perhaps Ann Summers parties should start by getting someone to ask each time, "Is There Anybody There?" Obviously, it could give an unusual twist to the whole occasion!

Chapter Four

SHORT BUT FUNNY STORIES

Here are a few short, sweet, laughable – and hopefully enjoyable – stories which I hope will bring a smile to everyone's face.

Many messages passed by a medium to members of church congregations or people attending public demonstrations can be amusing even when very brief, and can be enjoyed by everyone listening even though they are intended for just one person in particular. Listeners' imaginations can colour the message in such a way that everyone is laughing. Grandmothers, when communicating from spirit, can be not only loving, but also very funny. One night when I was working alongside John, who is a psychic artist, we found ourselves linking with the grandmother of a young lady in the audience. I was relaying clairvoyance related to the pictures John was drawing and, as he drew a portrait, the young lady in question recognised it as her grandmother – who told John that she had false teeth but didn't want the picture to show her wearing them. The audience was amused by this, but even more by what followed. The old lady wanted me to ask her granddaughter about a budgie, and I asked if Grandma had had one. "Not really", said her granddaughter, "I had promised to get her one, but never got around to it". To a gale of laughter, the old lady replied, "Tell her not to bother now; I have plenty up here to pick from and whatever colour I like!" As you can see, this special lady was just as sharp in spirit as she was on the earth-plane, and made sure that she had the last word on the subject.

The same evening I got into difficulties about someone's father, wrongly thinking he had told me something which, in fact, had been passed to me by a different relative. I described the character of a lady's father and gave her his name, which she confirmed as being correct, and I passed on details about events happening in the family. I was then told to tell her that her lovely cat was in spirit but hadn't been there very long and she said, "Yes, nearly a year now". Without hesitation, I was told to say, "You didn't have him doctored when he was on the earth-plane, did you?", which amused everyone, particularly when, after the lady said, "No", the communicator jauntily replied, "Well he has been now!" Unfortunately, the lady receiving this message said that she didn't think

James, her father, would have said this and I therefore checked with James for an explanation. Back came the reply, "George said it" and the lady confirmed that this was her brother in spirit and the message was just the kind of humourous remark he would make. It taught me to double-check on who is saying what in communication, so it "put me in my place", but is a good example of how the important animals in our lives are met and cared for by our family in spirit when they have left us here.

Sometimes our amusement is mixed with sadness, but it does not spoil the hilarity of funny situations. At one time I received a lovely letter from a very elderly lady in the town where I live. She had read a book of mine and asked whether, as she was housebound, I would be willing to visit her at home to give her a sitting. It was obvious from the way she used the telephone that she was very deaf, but we managed to understand, each other, and I agreed to call on her. As she lived on her own, I was instructed to open the porch door, take out a key from the sideboard drawer and proceed to the very top of the house. The very large, three-storey house had obviously been elegant in its day, but had not for a long time received the attention it needed and, as I went to meet her, I wondered what to expect, passing on the way antique furniture which had once been beautiful.

On entering the room, there sat the elderly lady in an armchair, completely surrounded by tables and chairs piled high with old newspapers, magazines and old plants. I introduced myself and explained to her how I worked. I then began to communicate with her husband and family in spirit. I had no sooner started than she said, "Wait a minute; I can't hear very clearly" and proceeded to pull out from beside her chair a home-made hearing aid consisting of two plastic funnels and a piece of rubber tubing. It was very hard not to start laughing and it must have looked hilarious to anyone watching from spirit as I proceeded to talk through the funnel on one end as she listened through the other, but nonetheless the sitting lasted for over an hour and she was thrilled with it.

Cartoon by Terence Carter

It appears that her husband was a well-known dignitary of great standing and it was sad to say this lovely lady, well into her eighties, living alone in the great building with only her daily help to visit her apart from an occasional visit from a nephew. I did visit her once more before she passed peacefully into spirit where she is now reunited with her loved ones.

I felt very sad about this lady being reduced to such a situation and living surrounded by so much paper and neglected antiques, but she was happy there even if all she had left were her happy memories of times long past.

Laughter is very much part of our work with spirit. At one recent demonstration, I was linking a young lady with her grandmother. After giving information regarding her home, her husband – who was with her and details about the fact that he wanted to be self-employed, all of which was accepted, the Grandmother asked me to enquire whether the young woman still had something which had belonged to her. "Yes", came the answer, and quick as lightning came a question about a picture. The granddaughter laughed and replied, "It's a picture of my grandmother; it's in the bedroom and I've hidden it behind the wardrobe!" Everyone laughed and the grandmother assured her that, if she wanted to get rid of it, she could, but her granddaughter assured her that she would not do so. I did wonder whether, on her return home, the picture would be resurrected and put somewhere visible or whether this lovely grandmother would remain for ever hidden behind the wardrobe.

Obviously, even though she is still not physically here, she has a good idea of what goes on in her absence, and could still make everyone smile.

THE DOG AND THE BRICKS

Other people's expectations can make life difficult for the medium to work fluently, particularly at public demonstrations. Often, it is expected that a medium will keep within specified guidelines and be "just so" in his presentation of messages. This is all very well, but when confronted with a spirit communicator who is very different from that, having a strong character, a ready use of vernacular speech and expecting the medium to relay messages in his own words, life can be quite difficult to stage manage!

Over the last few years, I have tried to contain such situations by expressing the words of my lovely spirit communicators in a language, not quite so blunt, but which keeps everybody happy.

Last year, I was booked to serve a particular Derbyshire church for the first time. It was to be a special evening of mediumship, with the psychic artist, John Brett, and I working alongside each other. As we were booked to do private sittings before the evening demonstration, we arrived at lunchtime and were greeted warmly and made to feel at home. The afternoon flowed by with everyone happy with their communication from spirit and we were therefore very much looking forward to working with such a nice atmosphere during the evening service.

Following a welcome break for a delicious meal provided by the church and the pleasant company of some committee members, we prepared for the evening demonstration. The church was very well attended and the atmosphere positive which was encouraging as this was hopefully the first of many visits to our new friends in Derbyshire, and naturally we wanted to make a good impression.

Following our introduction, I explained how I work and John had given his interpretation of his own work, so we were then ready to begin.

The evening got off to a very good start, as the first message was very emotional and relevant to the lady concerned, being from her husband who had recently passed to spirit, and concerning an important and very positive message about the situation regarding their house. It was obvious that spirit were, as usual, communicating with their usual love and guidance. A few more messages followed to be greeted with acceptance, laughter and love.

After this, I knew I was to go to a young lady right at the back of the church with messages from her mother and father who had left for the world of spirit when she was very young. They wanted to wish her a happy birthday for the next day and went on to tell her they knew of their grandchildren who had arrived after their passing, telling her about their own progress and that they continued to watch over them. They talked to their daughter about her house and mentioned that she had two Alsation dogs. All this was being accepted with some emotion by the young woman and at this moment, her father butted in and told me to say that she had not yet had the dogs doctored. To this, she answered, "No" and, before I knew it, the next words were out; I said, "Your father is showing me two bricks. Do you understand what he means?" To this, everyone started laughing and, as the laughter subsided, quite clearly from the congregation came this man's voice remarking, "Hope we are not going to start giving smutty messages now!" and the atmosphere, for a brief moment, froze.

Although I was aware of his remark, Spirit quickly said, "Do not retaliate, but continue with the message and keep the laughter going", so I did. Inwardly, however, I was now slightly apprehensive and thought, "That is that! We shall not be invited back here again." Spirit took away my fears, however, and the evening continued with more positive, happy messages.

I assumed that the person who had spoken was perhaps a member of the church or even on the committee, but felt that everyone else appeared to have enjoyed the evening and this was later confirmed, although it appeared that the man who made the remark was a new visitor to the church and was apparently unwell and not to be blamed for it. The spirit world would not have allowed me to pass on the message if it would have offended the daughter of my communicators; the father obviously knew this and it was obvious that her sense of humour was like his own.

After the service came to an end, everyone collecting pictures from John said how much they had enjoyed the evening, but I was still conscious of this disruptive remark and was awaiting a possible reprimand from the committee. Earlier we had accepted another booking for 1996 and I even wondered whether that would be cancelled but I was wrong. The gentleman apologised and the committee expressed the hope that it had not put me off coming to serve their church again. We accepted with pleasure.

In spite of such happenings, I have to accept that spirit is natural and the messages from spirit are normally to be given off as passed from them. If we try to alter their words or meanings, they will not be able to use us as a communicator between the two worlds.

I hope I have learned something from this and other similar experiences and realise that not everyone is going to like, or be able to accept, the way in which I work with spirit, but I am always delighted when, at the end of a demonstration, someone comes up to me and says, "That's just them! That's exactly how they would talk and say those things." Then I know I've done my job and Spirit are happy.

The final end to the evening was when the lady who received the message from her husband at the beginning of the evening came up and gave me a big hug, and said, "Thanks for something special", adding that she couldn't wait to get home and tell her son what his Dad had said.

I went home satisfied, knowing that, even though someone had been offended by my way of working with spirit, this lady had taken away all my doubts and worries as to whether I should change my way of working.

So often, I've been heard to say, "That's it! I'm not working spiritually any more." but I know in reality that I always will be communicating with spirit, bringing people love and laughter from their special people now living in the spirit world.

"OOPS", GET OUT OF THAT!

This chapter relates to situations such as when a medium, working from the platform, is left in an embarrassing situation even though they have felt in control of their spirit communicator.

I have not often been left with egg on my face whilst demonstrating in a church or larger venue, but it has been known to happen!

Most times, such situations are silly but amusing episodes – as have happened on occasion to me – like those when I have mistakenly said, "Can I come to the lady at the back with the red (or whatever colour) top?" only to be greeted by a lengthening silence, followed by a deep voice questioning, "Do you mean me?"

This amuses everyone, whilst I do my best to wriggle out of my mistake. Nowadays, with people wearing their hair long and sporting colourful, unisex clothes, the mistakes which are so easy to make are normally accepted in a friendly manner even if they result in banter for the person involved and laughter being directed at the somewhat embarrassed medium.

There can also be the unfortunate slip-up with many mediums, including myself, mostly in the early days of my spiritual work, where a dreaded swear-word has slipped out during a church demonstration on occasion – never a really bad one, but resulting sometimes in a reprimand from the chairperson or church committee! I have tried to ensure that my communicators do not get me into trouble, but I haven't always totally succeeded.

I am sure you all know by now that when we move into spirit we do not change out of all recognition, and many communicators talking to their loved ones via a medium talk exactly as they would have done when they were here on the earth-plane and that includes the swear words they were in the habit of using then.

In a one-to-one sitting, it is, I consider, permissible to use exactly the language they wish to communicate with. However, when working on a platform in public, it is definitely better to edit the presentation to convey what is said by saying that the person when on the earth-plane, would have used "colourful language" which the medium is unable to repeat. This usually brings lots of laughter from the person receiving the message who understands exactly, and also from the rest of the congregation or audience who put their own interpretation on the message and what the words might actually be. Although I have been in such a situation on the odd occasion with a swear-word escaping before I managed to screen it out, the worst faux-pas I have ever experienced happened to me recently. Although I laughed about it afterwards, at the time I wished the floor would open up and I could disappear.

The church involved was one I have attended over a number of years. Cambridge Avenue Spiritualist Church at Peterborough is a friendly and relaxed church to serve and, in the past, I have always been able to give good evidence there, with lots of laughter throughout an enjoyable evening. On Friday, July 5th 1996, it was a special evening of mediumship and the church was three-quarters full. After being welcomed to the platform by the chairperson, the service was handed over to me. Following the opening prayer, I explained how I work, explaining that it was a two-way communication and asking listeners to respond aloud, and that, this being so, we should get along fine. The serious work then followed as we joined the spirit world and our own. Very quickly the messages flowed. Spirit communicators were accepted and their information greeted with love and laughter.

It was a lively night and several communicators were gentlemen who would have pooh-poohed spiritual things when they were here. You can always tell as soon as you link with the voice of a spirit communicator if they are still having fun and pulling the legs of their family and friends about what is going on in their life. Such a gentleman was one I was receiving information from who was relating to his wife and daughter evidence of how he left and talking about his son and grandchildren and how Darren was always having his hair done. The spirit gentleman was enjoying himself and getting laughter in response as his wife agreed that Darren's hair was done every three weeks.

He then said to his wife something about someone going on holiday in a caravan shortly. This turned out to be his sister-in-law who was actually sitting a few rows in front of his wife. He decided to pull her leg and said that he would be coming on holiday with her and her husband when they went – and also when she played Bingo, which she confirmed she would be doing. He said he would be there, "nosing" as he put it and talked about her false teeth, telling her to take care of them whilst she was away on holiday as she hadn't a spare set. (I look forward to finding out what happened to them during the holiday, when I next visit.) The whole communication flowed with lots of love and laughter and had set the tone of the evening which appeared to be well on target to go particularly well. My next message was, however, for a young couple from the young man's grandfather. The grandfather had not been known to his grandson on the earth-plane, but he was keen to show his interest in their life. Information about a house move was readily accepted by the young people and I passed on information about their getting a dog. They agreed that they had been discussing this and we chatted about the fact that, though invisible, the grandfather was obviously part of their life. This led on to the next message about the garden, which the young man said needed sorting out and I was promptly shown a spade. In passing on this information, I began to say, "Your grandfather tells me, you need a spade" and meant to add, "and you also need a fork". Very unfortunately, it appears that is not what came out of my mouth!

What came out was, "Your grandfather tells me you need a spade and you also need a f..." I was in absolute honesty totally unaware of what I had said. Everyone burst into laughter at the bewilderment on my face. I had unconsciously allowed the communicator to express what he meant but it is a word I would never allow through in a demonstration and, although no-one appeared offended and were creased up with laughter, I really squirmed with embarrassment.

I apologised profusely to the young couple, the chairperson and to the church president who was sitting in the congregation, asking whether I was allowed to continue the demonstration but was assured that I could carry on and would, nonetheless, be invited back again in spite of everything.

I completed the demonstration which went well, with me trying to ensure that I made no more faux-pas that night and, with a few more apologies repeated later, began to feel a little less guilty about my experience even though I was greatly annoyed with myself for having allowed the situation to occur.

It did bring a smile to my face, however, when a lady came up to me after the demonstration and said, "Next time you make a mistake like that, can you speak up louder because my mother-in-law, sitting next to me, missed what you said and kept wanting to know why everyone was laughing so much". At least everyone knew no offense was meant but I doubt whether I shall ever live it down, particularly as my manager was there and said he would make sure my friends would all hear about it.

I did tell all the people at Cambridge Avenue that it would have to be included in my next book, so I hope they will enjoy hearing about the event from my side of the story.'

THE COCKATOO

This little story dates from my first visit to Ireland in March 1995. John and I had been invited to serve the Belfast Spiritualist Church during a 10-day visit. It proved to be a beautiful place and the people could not have been more friendly or spiritual. It was a very busy time filled with demonstrations, sittings, a workshop and the Sunday services.

The church was very well attended for our first Sunday evening service with over a hundred people present. We wondered what sort of reception our mediumship would receive, as for most of those present, it was their first experience of our work, but we need not have been concerned; it was a great night.

One incident which stands out in my memory concerned two sisters, one of whom was attending the church for the first time, and who sat apart in the front row of the congregation.

Their mother, who had just passed from cancer, came to talk to them, bringing along with her their father who had left for spirit many years previously at the young age of 42 years. This information was accepted by the daughters, whose parents continued with family memories and so on. As the contact began to draw to an end, however, their mother mentioned that she had a bird in spirit with her. I thought that this was a budgie, which puzzled the sisters who could not place such a bird at all. One of the ladies commented, "I have a cockatoo at home and that's all right", so I said, "Well, I don't know what your mother means, but she insists that she has a bird in spirit with her", and that was the end of the communication.

Two days later, one of the sisters came to see me for a private sitting and her first words to me were, "You remember you mentioned on Sunday about the bird in spirit? ..... Well, when I got home from the service, the cockatoo was dead!" Her mother was right; it must have arrived in spirit whilst they were in church, so spirit once again was proved to be "on the ball". At least, when her daughter got home and found the bird, she could be certain it was already being looked after by her parents in spirit.

I'm Very Well Thank You

There is nothing the matter with me,
I'm as healthy as I can be,
I have arthritis in both my knees,
Add when I talk – I talk with a wheeze.
My pulse is weak, and my blood is thin,
But – I'm awfully well for the shape I'm in.
Arch supports I have for my feet,
Or I wouldn't be able to be out on the street,
Sleep is denied me night after night,
But every morning I find I'm all right.
My memory is failing, my head's in a spin,
But – I'm awfully well for the shape I'm in.
The moral is this – as my tale I unfold,
That for you and me who are getting old,
It's better to say 'I'm fine' with a grin,
Than to let folks know the shape we are in.
How do I know that my youth is all spent?
Well, my 'get up and go' has got up and went.
But I really don't mind when I think with a grin,
Of all the grand places my 'got up' has bin.
Old age is golden I've heard it said,
But sometimes I wonder as I get into bed,
With my ears in a drawer, my teeth in a cup,
My specs on a table until I get up.
'Ere sleep overtakes me I say to myself,
Is there anything else I could lay on the shelf?
When I was young my slippers were red,
I could kick my heels right over my head,
When I was older my slippers were blue,
But I still could dance the whole night through.
Now I am old my slippers are black,
I walk to the shop and puff my way back,
I get up each morning and dust off my wits,
And pick up the paper to read the 'obits',
If my name is still missing I know I'm not dead;
And so I have breakfast and – go back to bed.

Author unknown.

Chapter Five

WITHIN THE HOUR

This very short story is proof that spirit can show that people or animals can communicate instantly after their passing.

The evening of August 4th 1996 was one of those rare occasions on which I was serving my local spiritualist church at Sleaford – rare because, being my local church, I prefer not to serve there as a medium on a regular basis as I know so many of those who attend. However, I had agreed to work there that evening in place of a medium who had cancelled a booking.

The church was nice and full both with regular attenders and some new people and, as the evening progressed, we reached the time of spiritual communication which so many people look forward to. As the demonstration began, everything was happily being accepted with the usual love and laughter which are so much part of it.

I think it was the third message given in which I was drawn to a lady dressed in blue, who spirit wished to speak with. On telling the lady that her father wished to send his love and to say, "Hello" which she accepted, I passed on a few more words about the family memories. I then said to the lady, "Are you a cat person? I have one here in spirit with your father." She sadly replied, "Yes; it only died one hour ago, just before we came to church. It was run over." The lady's father assured her it was okay, then described a tabby cat which apparently was another cat which had disappeared at the same time. This lovely lady had apparently lost two cats in the previous hour but her father did his best to reassure her that they were all right, telling her that the one with him was well and purring in spirit.

It just goes to show that animals are also important and when they arrive in spirit are also met by our family, loved and comforted, and still part of our family life.

Chapter Six

THE LADY OF THE HOUSE

In 1984, I made a choice which changed my life. Having spent the previous 25 years living in the county of Kent, I decided to leave everything there behind and return to my roots in Lincolnshire. Since my many friends were in Kent, the fact that I had family in Lincolnshire did not mask the feeling that I was leaving for the "unknown". In a sense I was, but the reason for the choice did not emerge until about two years later. Whilst looking for suitable accommodation to rent, the modern places I viewed "left me cold", until I visited a vacant flat in the village which the agents agreed to show me somewhat unwillingly, as they didn't feel it would be what I wanted. They took me to an old farmhouse which was divided into two flats, the vacant one overlooking a barn, crewyard and paddock at the back of the house. The peace seemed to surround me and, as I walked into the house, it was just as if I knew I had to live there and promptly applied for the tenancy.

    I moved into Mount Lane Farm on November 5th 1984, never dreaming what lay ahead for me.

Mount Lane Farm

On settling into my new home, I felt as if I had always lived there and my past seemed a long way behind me. However, of all the rooms in the house, I was most aware of the bedroom overlooking the orchard in which I never felt relaxed and could not sleep. I thought it was just that I preferred the other bedroom but the true reason became clear in May 1986 when, for the first time, I was made aware of my spiritual gift. Following this discovery, I had decided to use this particular room as the one I would sit in for meditation to link up with my guide, Running Foot, with whom I had just become acquainted. During the time I spent in this bedroom, I gradually became aware of a presence within the room of a lady who seemed to be linking up with me. She appeared to me to be elderly and wearing a long black dress and a white lace cap on her head and to have trouble with her legs. I always felt pain in my own legs whenever she

Mrs Mastin (Grace)

appeared and she always seemed to attract my attention to the windows as if she would spend a lot of time looking out of them into the orchard. On getting more curious, I began to ask the lady questions as to who she was and in response I became aware of the name "Grace" followed by "Mastin" and the information that she lived here and was part of the farm.

As by then I knew Tom, the owner of the farm, I gently probed about this lady when I saw him and he was very helpful which was a relief as, at that time, nobody knew of my spiritual gift and I didn't want to upset anyone or be asked to leave. However, Tom listened as I explained about the clothes and appearance and responded, "Yes. That's Mrs Mastin whose husband owned the farm." He added, "I have some photos of them; I'll show you them," which he did the following week.

I then knew that Mrs Mastin had definitely been communicating with me as her image in the photograph was exactly as I had been shown her during the first week of my awareness.

Naturally, now I had found something so special and fascinating, I wanted to know much more, and began to ask more questions of this new lady in my life. Grace made me aware of her desire for me to take a pen and write down her answers. Since, although I had never experienced such a thing, I had heard of automatic writing, I thought, "Well, why not?" and proceeded to hold the pen lightly on the paper whilst asking Grace questions. She would scrawl back the answers. I still have them in my possession.

Mrs Mastin, or Grace as she now likes to be called, wanted to go with me to the church on the other side of the village to see where she was now resting. On visiting the churchyard to see the grave for the first time, I felt myself being directed to a row of gravestones with the name Mastin on each one. I couldn't see any with the name Grace Mastin on, but felt drawn to one bearing the name Frederick Mastin above the name of his wife, Mary Ann, who died on May 25th 1938 aged 97, which seemed strange as it was also the year of my own birth.

On returning home, I commented to Grace that she had told me a fib, as her name was not Grace. She quickly replied, "My real name is Mary Ann but I liked to be called Grace; I did not tell a fib," and continued by thanking me for taking her to the church. On again mentioning the matter to Tom, he confirmed that she was known as Mrs Mastin to him and everyone he knew as a child but that to her very special friends she was always known as Grace, as she was very strict and proper about her position in life. It was obviously a privilege to know that I was classed as being amongst her special friends and I felt Grace knew that I would not abuse her thoughts or things she might choose to show me during the next period of my progression in the things relating to the spirit world.

In one of the many conversations between us which followed, Grace asked of me a special favour. She wished to show me something at the bottom of the farm and she directed me towards a derelict building and some old farm implements. Grace had me removing old rotten wood and rubbish until I unearthed some very old horse straps bearing small brass buckles which I removed and brought back to the house for cleaning. Obviously Grace had known they had been buried there years before. I felt that this was her way of giving me more proof of her awareness of still being part of life at the farm and what was happening on it, realising that through me Grace had found an outlet for her awareness too.

She would often ask me if we could go to the church together and we would go and sit inside – always at the same pew where the stained glass window was in full view. It was so peaceful. I always felt as if I had gone back through the years and was sitting with Grace at the era when she would have attended church. The peace and calmness felt was wonderful and I would always come back minus worries and fears and with a renewed urge to progress with my spirit work.

After years now of spiritual awareness, Grace is still a very important person in my life. She often makes her presence felt, occasionally coming into a room while I am giving a sitting but usually she doesn't stay for long. I have to smile often when this happens, as people frequently say how cold their legs have become or as if one side of them has gone icy cold, even in summer. Sometimes I explain about Grace's visits, but more often I pass it off with an excuse. Not everyone is capable of accepting the company of a spirit person in the house and would be alarmed if they knew, so I have to know when to say anything and when not.

Early on in my work, a group of girls visited me regularly for sittings and they knew about Grace. One of them would never visit the upstairs "loo" and would rather suffer until she went home. Often people refuse to go upstairs on their own and it's funny to watch them all troop up there together.

Looking back over everything that happened at the time, it was very obviously the work of spirit to place me in an environment where my spiritual awareness could be discovered and where I was provided with the special friendship of Grace who left the earth plane for the spirit world in the year when I was born into the world where now this special gift can be used, linking those in the spirit world with their loved ones here on earth. They are indeed just a touch away.

Chapter Seven

THE SPIRIT WORLD

There are many conflicting ideas about what the spirit world is like. People read descriptions in journals and books, and have conversations with those who claim to know what the world beyond physical death is like, and become very confused.

According to what I have been told by my guides and those members of the world of spirit who talk to me and to their loved ones during sittings at my home, we can learn a lot about it.

Everything is made up of energy and, while we are living on the earth plane, we contain our energy field within a physical body. When we no longer need that physical body, we discard it to join those in the spirit world. The energy field which is us – our individual spirit – moves free of our separated physical body and on to better things, able to relate to others in the world of spirit and also, when the conditions are right, to those of us still here on the earth plane.

When I link up with those who have left us for the spirit world, their energy joins up with mine, sometimes making me feel like a battery "on charge". I regard them as being like bright lightbulbs, their energy and mine together joining with their loved ones to make a strong connection between the different levels of life.

The levels with which I communicate are worlds of feeling and thought, and our loved ones present what they wish to say to us in ways which we can understand. If I were to say to most people that I was talking to a bright light, or an energy field, they would find it very difficult to understand and might be afraid, but communicators often refer to "drinking a pint" or "smoking" and habitually give off images which refer precisely to their normal behaviour patterns while they were on earth, enabling their loved ones to recognise them easily.

When we leave this material world behind for the world of spirit, we no longer have a body which needs to feed or rest, leaving behind earthly restrictions which limit us. On a spiritual level, we can develop and progress in knowledge and understanding acquiring insight which we did not have before.

Therefore, those who speak to us from the spirit world, bring a combination of their earth-learning and the understanding they have acquired in the higher worlds, which puts them in a good position to try to help us to expand our own awareness both of constructive ways of behaving to each other down here, and of prompting us to understand the meaning of life and the importance of love.

There is often much frustration amongst those in the spirit world because they long to do more for the earth in bringing peace and harmony to unite those in conflict, but because we on this level have freedom of choice to decide our actions, only we can create that peace and harmony. Sadly, our greedy obsession with material things and our yearning for power make the achievement of this goal very difficult.

The day would seem to be long gone when life was simple, when natural food and farming methods and providing for one's own needs was the order of the day and when we made our own enjoyment and entertainment. The population explosion and man's progress over the past years has created a far more complicated world. We have created our own destiny, but life is cyclic and maybe the coming generations will be a little wiser, more knowledgeable, and less greedy, so that the many life-forms on earth will be able to live in joyous harmony and love.

People have varied attitudes to this work which we do. Some are warmly supportive and accept our gift of spirit communication, whilst others are extremely opposed to it and try to prove that the work is "of the devil". I find such attitudes very sad, as most people holding them have never bothered to investigate what we do before condemning it. They feel justified in trying to pass their comments about us to others even so, based entirely on what they have heard or read of other people's opinions.

I accept everyone's freedom of choice and know that those whom I can help will come to see me.

A person's voice is, for me, an important link with Spirit. Once I hear the vibrations of a voice, I know whether a speaker really needs help or not. One lady who telephoned me prompted me to question her reasons for calling; even whilst I was talking to her, I felt curious, but tried to disregard my unease.

In answer to her queries, I explained how I work giving evidence of spirit survival. She wanted me to book sittings for herself and two friends, but specified three separate sittings at 2.30 pm on different days. I only ask for first names of sitters, so wrote their names in the relevant diary slots, but was aware that it was a little odd that the caller had neither asked the cost nor where I lived. The phone call over, Spirit impressed me with the fact that all was not right, and I underlined the names with the date of the booking and a question mark and a note to the effect that they would not turn up. I thought that if Spirit were right, then I would get some rest time. Running Foot gave me the feeling that these ladies' religious leanings had prompted them to try to take booking space to prevent others using it.

When July arrived, Spirit were proved right. None of the ladies either turned up or cancelled, but it did enable me to deal with some other important business and I was able to see a young man who needed help urgently instead. He telephoned me one day Just before 2.30 pm and I was able to see him immediately to give him the help he so much needed, so none of us lost out.

Even when someone turns up in place of the person who actually booked in for the sitting, they are often shaken by my remarking, "Is So-and-So with you?" It never bothers me when a substitute sitter turns up, as the person arriving often needs spirit help at that time which couldn't wait until later, but visitors are sometimes startled that I can tune in so easily. It makes me understand that many people are wary of me on occasion, but that I accept as part of my chosen pathway, working with Spirit.

Chapter Eight

THE KNOCKS AND DOUBTS

There are many misunderstandings about being a medium. Some of the stories which come back to us are astonishing. Sometimes they make me smile and wonder how on earth they could have arisen. Others are sad. Because of the work mediums do, different people see us in various ways; some see us as working for the devil, whilst others think of us as weird people in darkened rooms lit only by flickering candles and with incense burning. Others come expecting us to focus our attention on a crystal ball, and others avoid us like the plague because they think we can read their minds, and then there are those who think we have a mental disorder because they think we are talking to ourselves. It is sad that such misconceptions still exist and I hope that by writing about the working of spirit, people will become more aware of the truth and feel free to come themselves to communicate with their own loved ones.

One of the most amazing stories which found its way back to my ears concerned a situation which is supposed to have taken place at my home. It appears that, when some people told their neighbours that they were coming for a sitting, the neighbours answered, "I wouldn't if I were you. Didn't you hear of what happened when two sisters went to see that medium? After he gave them a sitting, he went into another room and after a while, he came back with a sealed envelope and gave it to one of the sisters, telling her not to open it until they got home. On the way home, the sisters were killed in a dreadful car accident and, when the family opened the envelope, there was just a blank piece of paper inside, so he obviously knew they were going to die!" This story was told me by more than one sitter who came to see me at different times from the particular village concerned, but to date none has been able to provide any evidence of the ladies' home or any such accident. As the village is only a few miles away, it certainly would have made the news and the story seems to have become more alarming each time it was told. It appears that the person who originated it was very religious and it would seem the story was designed to frighten people away from coming into connection with us.

Many people relate similar stories to me of how a friend, neighbour, or family member has tried to deter them from linking with their loved ones in spirit, believing that it is "the work of the devil". Some even go to the extreme of refusing to have any more to do with the person if they do come for a sitting. However, the sitters always say that the peace of mind they have found through coming has made the hassle worthwhile. The people who are afraid mostly do not know what they are missing. They are really indoctrinated into believing other people's attitudes and it is a pity they have not the understanding or courage to come and see for themselves. Then they would be free to judge and make comment from their own experience.

Within my own family, one family member who is a Jehovah's Witness, on hearing of my mediumship, told the others that they must have nothing more to do with me as I was evil. Thank goodness, my family and friends know me better and, although some of them do not believe in Spirit, know that I have freedom of choice to do my chosen work, desiring to help and guide those who freely come to visit me, and recognising both their and my rights to our own beliefs without being condemned for them.

I have even been told that sitters have been forewarned not to accept a drink of tea or coffee before we begin, in case I put something in to get them "under my spell" and unaware of what happens to them while they are there! Perhaps someone might like to tell me what that would be; I certainly do not know.

At one time, I gave a sitting to a lady who confirmed that all the information given off was correct, saying it was her father who had communicated, and asking to bring her brother at a later date for a second sitting. On the second occasion, I refused to charge them for the two hours I had spent trying to relate, as the information was disastrously spasmodic and disjointed. My apologies notwithstanding, they were nonetheless very disappointed, particularly as it transpired that the date would have been her father's birthday and the lady had hoped to hear of his pleasure about her own pregnancy.

Among the letters on display at my home is the one the lady wrote to me at that time quoting her friend's opinion that I had perhaps hypnotised her and read her mind on the first visit and been prevented from doing so when she returned by her brother's presence on that occasion.

I politely replied, telling her that I am unable to hypnotise anyone, nor do I work that way, and suggesting that perhaps it would be better in the future if she were to sit with another medium to get the results she was looking for.

It is useful, I feel, to be able to display both supportive and sceptical letters about my work, so that people can make up their own minds about it. As I see it, my job is to show to the best of my ability that there is life beyond this material plane to look forward to, and that our loved ones who are "just a touch away" are able to communicate their knowledge, guidance and love from their world which is just beyond this one.

Chapter Nine

OBSTACLES

Some of the most difficult situations I, as a medium, have to deal with involve religious fanatics. In general, the Church of England and the Roman Catholic Church intend to keep a low profile about spiritualism, even if they do not agree with it, but "Born Again Christians", "Jehovah's Witnesses" and members of "New-Life Churches" tend to feel a need to picket demonstrations of mediumship and quote extracts from the Bible in the press against our work.

I find this sad as, in spite of supposedly being Christians, they seem committed to creating and stirring up trouble.

We can all quote the Bible by taking extracts out of context to prove a point and it has become routine for them to quote Deuteronomy against mediumship – a book which is part of the Old Testament, the holy book of Judaism. However, I am frequently surprised that Christians so seldom quote from their own New Testament, the book of Jesus and his followers, which contains specifically Christian teaching i.e. I Corinthians chapter 12, vv 4–10, where the wise St Paul (the Roman Jew of Tarsus who converted to Christianity) speaks of spiritual gifts through Christ.

Maybe the Born-Again Christians etc have not read the rest of the Old Testament which contains a vast amount of material which is shocking and cruel even by our 20th Century standards. Why quote just one verse which suits an argument and forget the other?

No matter how much ranting and raving religious people of whatever persuasion may do, people will still think for themselves and will choose their own pathways. In fact, whenever such people create adverse publicity for me, I find that it draws more people to hear me, especially at public demonstrations, as they come to see for themselves what is going on.

Fanatics of all kinds will always be around, but will never be able to keep people from searching for their own idea of God or beliefs which match their own truth. Nowadays people do not like to be told what to do or think. This is why many people are surprised to find that, in investigating Spiritualism, when they come to find out what is on offer, there is the freedom to listen to the communication with spirit, to consider it and to question its accuracy, and whether it is appropriate or not for them. If not, then they can easily move on to search for another way of finding help to meet their needs and finding peace with themselves and with God.

However, that is not the only kind of intrusive behaviour with which mediums have to deal. There are also people who visit a medium for other reasons of their own. They may have family in spirit, but deep down are wanting the medium to make decisions for them, rather than wanting to take responsibility for their own choices, knowing that, if they themselves make a particular choice, then the responsibility is their own, but if someone in spirit (or the medium) suggests a particular course of action and it works out badly, then they can always say, "It wasn't my fault . . . so-and-so told me to do it!"

When I give a private sitting, I like to have it taped because people's memories and understanding of what any medium says can change drastically over a period of time, especially when telling other folks what was said. As I try to make clear in my sittings, messages passed to me come from people in spirit who give evidence of their being who they say they are, enabling the sitter to accept them with confidence, and to hear what they have to say. The messages are not from me, just from their loved ones in spirit.

Thankfully, over the years I have been working, I know that the majority of sitters have enjoyed and accepted what has been given as proof of spirit communication, but understand that the information is for them to think about and then, at the end of the day, include in their considerations when they make their own decisions about what to do in their lives. Unfortunately, this is not the way it works when people avoid taking personal responsibility for their lives. Then the medium is the greatest person alive if he has given advice which has pleased them – and the one first in the firing line if the choice made does not work out well. The medium is simply a communicator with spirit and with them. He is not there to make decisions for them. That is their job.

Personally, I do not charge a fee for sittings in which I feel I have not been able to establish positive communication or with which the sitter is unhappy. In such circumstances, I advise them to see another medium who may be better able to help them.

The more a medium becomes known and his reputation well thought-of, the more is expected of him and it is not always possible to please everyone.

I remember one sitting I gave for a couple who had come for a return visit. Obviously, they had previous experience of my work and felt it worth coming again. The sitting took much longer than the usual appointment. In fact, I worked with them for nearly two hours; it was, as I remember it, somewhat difficult as the husband's father wanted to communicate and give his version of how he saw what was happening to his son and family, whereas the wife's family communicating from spirit, saw matters differently, and wished to make their views clear. All this was taped, and I explained that, although their loved ones in spirit had differing views, only they could decide what was right for them to do.

The communication was just guidance offered for them to consider. The two sitters commented that the wife's communicator from spirit was awkward and they understood why she would argue and differ from the husband's father, so, although I was not 100% happy with the sitting, I felt that having worked so hard, it was well worth the fee. Obviously they did not get what they came for, however, since I discovered later that, although spirit were focusing on their current problems with work and house-moves, it was actually their own spiritual development they wanted clarification about.

Having not charged extra for what was effectively a double sitting, I was surprised two weeks later to receive a letter from the wife saying that, when they got home, they found that only 15 minutes of the tape made sense and the rest was rubbish. She considered that I should not have charged for such a session and felt she should have her fee refunded plus a few other somewhat sarcastic comments. Without hesitation, I returned her fee with a polite letter telling her that obviously whatever she was looking for would probably have to come from another medium, and I wished her all the best with her search.

I would have preferred her to tell me straight away rather than waiting for two weeks before complaining especially since her husband appeared quite happy with everything said.

It is no good going to see a medium, if you are going to judge his ability to communicate with spirit on whether what is communicated suits you or not. Otherwise, no medium will be judged of any worth unless he tells you what you want to hear whether it is the truth or not!

Then again, I have to learn to cope with the odd person who telephones to leave a message on the answer machine with no name or telephone number to reply to. One man phoned up at 3.00 am stating that he had been at a demonstration the previous night which I had done for a charity, saying he thought the evening was a load of rubbish (except he put it more strongly!) and just rang off. It appears that he also phoned the organiser of the event saying that they must have made a packet of money and thought it was dreadful. To my mind, the man was either very odd, or just wanted to cause trouble for reasons of his own.

Recently, a lady left a message on the answer machine saying she "wanted to leave a message for Bryan", saying that I had destroyed her life with my clairvoyant prophecy and hoping that I can live with myself. She left no name or telephone number to contact her on, but strangely it did not distress me because I felt that this lady was not someone who had in fact had a sitting with me. Most people would have used the term "spiritual advice" or "spiritual message", not "prophecy". This is a word normally used by fundamentalist christians but, since I have no means of contacting her, the truth will have to remain unsure. If she had had a sitting, it would all have been on tape and she could have discussed it with me personally and allowed me to discuss it with her. These situations do worry me as I genuinely care about doing my best for my sitters and for Spirit. Over the years, I have tried to ensure that what is said is understood properly as being suggestions for consideration when they themselves come to make decisions about their lives not as instructions to be obeyed. People in spirit have lived their lives; these lives are ours and it is up to each of us to take responsibility for the choices we make, but some people still tend to want someone else to take the blame for the decisions they make which do not work out as they hope.

Even with many such difficulties, I know I shall always continue to work spiritually. Because all my work comes through recommendation of previous sitters, and I have worked hectically throughout the last ten years, I suppose I must be doing most things right in reaching out to those people who really do need the love and understanding from their loved ones, family and friends in spirit.

As one of my friends is always quoting, "Obstacles are opportunities for growth". Given the number of obstacles there are in this work, perhaps I shall start growing soon!

Chapter Ten

SOMETIMES, IT IS SO HARD TO BE A MEDIUM

So many people have serious reservations about spiritualism and the way in which mediums communicate, that people frequently come to see us simply to prove that they are right, we are wrong and probably a bit "batty" into the bargain.

I have come across many people who try to analyse my work and give theories for how the communications are given, suggesting that I provide messages by reading sitters' body language, that I make leading comments so that I can provide further information based on their responses whilst pretending that the messages come from spirit. Some people even believe that I go to great lengths to check up on people in advance and ascertaining their addresses and so on before speaking to them. For a start, if I did, I would never have time to give sittings and certainly the cost of doing such things would be beyond belief. When accused in such a way, it is difficult for me to keep my own counsel on occasions and refrain from retaliation, but to do so would only play into their court and I find it much better to not do so.

Recently such an incident occurred at a local church in Boston where naturally I know numerous people, but not as personal friends and not in such a way as to have access to details of their private lives; enough, nonetheless, to call some by their first names, certainly. However, that particular evening, most of the people attending were new to me and I assumed that, for many, it was their first time at the church.

As usual, when I arrived for the service, I kept out of the way and was unaware of people attending until I mounted the platform. At that point I was able to see both the regulars and the newcomers, as the service began.

After the opening prayer and a hymn, the spiritual communication got underway and I remember giving messages to two people whom I already had met previously at the church. I try to serve this particular church about once a year and so had not visited recently, and the messages which I relayed to them from their loved ones were gratefully received.

Frequently, particularly if I am giving a theatre demonstration, I make a point of saying that I am going to pass on a message to a particular person, even though I do know them, and that I am passing on what is being said for them in spite of the fact that I already have met them on a previous occasion. On this particular Sunday evening, that did not occur to me, unfortunately, and I continued to pass on a lot of messages being relayed to me from spirit for various members of the congregation. It was only when I eventually went to four ladies sitting together that I was in for a startling surprise.

The first of the four was a lady sitting at the end of the row, who emotionally accepted evidence from her husband in spirit who had passed in his 40s and who went on to give her the names of his brothers still here on the earth-plane, and saying that he was sad that, following his passing, the attitude of his family towards her had changed. He encouraged her to ignore this and to get on with her life, saying that he hoped this would help her. She said that it would; it was her first time in the church and her first message from her husband.

I still had with me another young man who had left through an accident and he directed me to talk to the young lady at the other end of the row. On asking her whether she could accept a young man in spirit who left life through an accident, she half-heartedly said, "Yes".

I continued to give her information from the young man, saying his name was Mark, his age was 21 and that he had worked in the building trade. He said he had just arrived in spirit. On asking whether she could accept all this, she rather aggressively said, "You have read that in the papers". This took me completely back, as there was no way in which I had read anything about this person and I promptly told her so. I tried, rather poorly in my shocked state, to explain to her about the communication, but I was so angry at being accused of presenting a non-genuine communication, that I attempted to compose myself, passed on a few more words from her grandmother in spirit, and concluded the message.

By now, the church was very still and quiet. Obviously everyone there was embarrassed as they could see my reaction, but fortunately I managed to not retaliate and to get on with other communicators.

As the evening wore on, I again relaxed and the atmosphere became pleasant again. After the service, many people came up to me and apologised for the unpleasantness and were supportive and kind.

However, I found it very difficult to get out of my mind, as I care far too much about my connection with spirit to do any such thing.

On thinking about the whole thing it is obvious that, even had I read about the accident in the paper, there is no reason why I should have known that the young man had anything remotely to do with her. The message was not thrown out to the congregation in general; the young man went straight to her, because he knew her – I think he had gone out with her, but as it was she missed out on what could have been a lovely evening full of love and laughter, linking with a special person in spirit who wished to communicate with her, so no doubt I should feel sorry for her rather than angry and offended by the incident. However, it did make me aware of how careful we have to be when dealing with people whose minds are not open to the truth of life after death.

Chapter Eleven

CLAIRE AND LINDSEY

Claire and Lindsey Stirling are two very special twin girls whose story began in my first book, "Life Beyond the Storm". Both little girls suffered from the illness called cystic fibrosis and finally lost their fight for life, leaving for the world of spirit when they were three years old. As I said at the time, such a loss is very hard for all of us to accept and I felt privileged to be involved in helping their family to come to terms with the loss of two of their daughters within the space of five months. Claire, the chatty one, left us on Easter Sunday in 1988 and her sister, Lindsey in July of the same year.

The story began on Easter Sunday that year with a phone call. The gentleman speaking to me on his car phone wanted urgent help for one of his employees whose little daughter had just lost her battle for life. He didn't really know why he was phoning me, but felt that perhaps I might be able to help.

A few evenings later, I sat with the lock of hair and dress sent to me by Claire's father and the little girl made contact with me. She appeared laughing, saying that she was at peace and free from the distress she had experienced on earth. She gave me details about her passing, and talked about her sister, telling me her name and when their birthday was, and saying that they would both have been four in September.

Claire's mother subsequently contacted me, thanking me for the information and saying it had helped them to cope with the loss of Claire; she also talked of the possibility of visiting me when it could be arranged. However, in the July, she telephoned again as Lindsey had deteriorated and had come home from hospital to spend the short time left to her on earth with her family.
During this conversation, Claire joined us. I could see her watching her sister lovingly and trying to bring strength and love to all the family in their difficulty. The twins' father spoke to me two days later, asking whether I knew how long Lindsey would live; although I was unable to tell him the answer to that question, I was able to reassure him that I knew Lindsey would soon be at peace and that Claire and Lindsey would be together again. It was the following week when this happened and the funeral took place on the Thursday. The twins'

Claire and Lindsey

parents and their remaining daughter, Jill, went away for a few days to spend time together and to start adjusting to their new situation and, on their return home, contacted me in their loneliness to make a date to come to see me.

Finally, Lorraine and Billy came down from Scotland to spend time with me in the September just after the anniversary of the twins' birthday.

I really had looked forward to meeting them and, having greeted them at the door, found myself feeling as if I had known them all my life. We had a brief chat and a cup of tea, but we were not alone. The girls could not wait to get on with the sitting and started chatting quite freely, giving names of members of their families and talking about their life in Scotland. It seemed only a short time that we were all talking together but, when we looked at the clock, we realised that three hours had passed. Although we were all reluctant to break the spirit communication with Claire and Lindsey, we knew that tomorrow would provide further time for sharing together.

On the Sunday morning as I was preparing breakfast, I felt that little Lindsey was trying to tell me something because I kept being made aware of my wrist. When looking at it, I saw a little, silver bracelet being placed on it which remained until the twins' father, Billy, came downstairs. He hardly had a chance to speak before the message for Billy was delivered. I asked him, "Did the girls have silver bracelets on their wrists when they were buried?" "Yes", he answered, "They did".

With that, Lindsey was quiet for a while and the girls seemed content now that I had given off this information. Following breakfast, we sat down once more at around 11 a.m., to link up with Claire and Lindsey to see what else they wanted to chat about. When the girls had given most of their news, Lorraine and

Billy wanted to know more about spiritualism and how it worked, hoping that they themselves might be able to understand not only how I managed to communicate with their daughters in the spirit world, but also how they might be able to do so also.

After Lorraine and Billy had returned home, I had a telephone call from Lorraine saying that they had been to take flowers to the girls' grave and that, for the first time, they had not felt sad at leaving as they knew that the girls were with them and it had helped them greatly.

In April 1989, I kept my promise to visit Bathgate in Scotland where the family lived, to meet up again with Lorraine and Billy and also to meet Jill, Claire and Lindsey's elder sister, for the first time.

On my arrival, I found I felt like a member of the family, not at all like a stranger, and the strong feeling of warmth which surrounded me was familiar as was the house itself. In the room where I was to sleep, I found two single beds and chose to sleep in the one nearer the door.

I awoke during the night to Lindsey talking, keeping me awake and very aware of her presence. Billy subsequently confirmed that the bed I had used had indeed been Lindsay's who obviously was determined that I should be aware of her presence and the distinction between her and Claire. Lots of lovely things happened that week; the girls were capable of being quite mischievous. Having watched a family video of a visit to Edinburgh Zoo taken before Claire's passing, I realised that they were strong characters here as well as in the spirit worlds.

At the end of a week of such hospitality I was sad to leave Scotland, but knew that I would return to spend more time with these people who treated me as one of their own family, and am glad that this proved to be so.

The telephone, however, is a good substitute at times when Lorraine and Billy are feeling low or needing spiritual reassurance; usually the girls have messages for them. On one occasion when their mother phoned, the girls gave me a message about a broken window. This reassured Lorraine that the girls were still in touch with the events of family life here on earth, since Billy's car had been broken into that week and the window smashed.

Although it is now some time since the twins' passing, obviously their parents still miss their physical presence, but their spiritual contact is a real comfort which helps them in their loss.

It was a pleasure when Lorraine phoned me to say that, as the girls had previously predicted, their father had just won a competition as top drummer at one of Scotland's Highland Games.

Lorraine, Billy and Jill still have the encouragement of the twins in the things they do, but most of all they still have their love.

Chapter Twelve

JANE AND CARL

In 1995 I promised to include this story in the new book, not knowing at the time that the lady I was making the promise to would by that time be in spirit herself.

That year, Jane and Lawrence visited me for the first time, having travelled from Scunthorpe for their sitting.

At the beginning of the sitting, explanations about the way I work over, I was made aware of their son in spirit. Information began to filter through, as he gave off his love, with communication about his baby son whom he was watching over. Although information was being accepted by the sitters, I was not all that happy as Carl, who had by then given me his name, still appeared to be agitated and stressed. I asked him to slow down and to give me more information to pass to his parents. I was given the feeling of being surrounded by water and Carl's next words were, "My Mum and Dad are unable to find me to bury me". On giving this information to Jane and Lawrence, Jane emotionally confirmed that Carl had jumped from the Humber Bridge and his body had never been found; the Police had by then given up searching as the event had taken place a year previously.

It did help Jane and Lawrence to know that he was alive in spirit and had come through to communicate in spite of the pain and uncertainty which remained, not knowing where his body was, nor being able to lay it to rest as they wanted to.

Once the atmosphere became more relaxed, Carl was able to provide more information about his girl-friend and the trouble which had caused him to take his own life. Carl also mentioned his brother, Craig, who was married with two sons named Mark and Paul, both of whom he was also taking an interest in. Carl wanted his family to know that he was all right and said he had his grandfather in spirit with him. He was sorry for all the trouble he had caused but was now at peace with himself.

At the end of the sitting, Jane bought my book, "Spirit, my Second Home" and said, "I hope you will include Carl's story in your next book as it may help others to understand and be comforted who have lost children in similar situations.

L. WARRINER
SCUNTHORPE
NORTH LINCS

DEAR BRYAN

I AM ENCLOSING ANOTHER PHOTO OF MY SON CARL WHICH YOU ASKED FOR THANK YOU FOR THE SITTING. I GOT TO KNOW QUITE A LOT, AS FOR JANES ASHES JANE MUST HAVE KNOWN I HAD THEM IN THE FLAT WITH ME WE ARE GOING ALONG WITH JANES WISHES TWO WEEKS TIME ON THE SUNDAY TWELVE MINUTS PAST 1 OCLOCK SAME TIME AS CARL LEFT US.
   THANK YOU BRYAN
          L. E. Warriner

Letter from Carl's mother

About four months later, I received a brief letter with a photograph of Carl and his baby son, as she had promised.

Because of pressures of work, I didn't think any more about getting down to writing about Carl and it was July 1996 before I was to communicate with Carl again.

The sitting was for two people, Lawrence and Allison. I was not aware of who they were and I began the sitting in the usual way as, although Lawrence said he had been before, his daughter-in-law said she had not. As the sitting began, the first communicator who came through was a lovely lady who stated that she had just passed into spirit very quickly whilst in hospital. This was accepted by the sitters and the lady confirmed that she was Lawrence's wife and wanted her love passed on. Then she continued to talk about her son who was also in spirit with her and wanted her family to know she was now happy. She had met her son and he was all right.

Carl Warriner with his son

Now the sitting was very positive, she decided to give me her son's name which she said was Carl and told me her name was Jane. She talked about the hospital and the quickness of her passing. Lawrence confirmed this and it appears that Jane had had a lung transplant which had taken, but Jane had just left without any warning and, at the time of the sitting, the results of the post-mortem were still awaited. However, at that time, Jane did give me the sensation of a heart attack, so confirmation of this is still awaited.

Jane talked more about her son, Craig, and Allison and the grandsons, Mark and Paul, and wanted her love passed to them.

At this point of the sitting, Jane talked about her funeral. She said that she had been cremated and that Lawrence was unsure where to put her ashes as she had not wanted to be buried. She asked for the ashes to be scattered on the water where Carl had left for the world of spirit, so that they could be joined together here as well as in spirit where they now are. Allison said that Craig had mentioned this and his mother confirmed that this was her wish and wanted Lawrence to talk this through with Craig and Allison.

We hope this story will help others to understand when they come up against tragic situations such as this. It illustrates the fact that people who love one another do meet up in the spirit world. Carl's body has not been recovered from the river, although it is certain that he jumped from the bridge as I believe it was caught on camera.

It is very difficult for families left behind in situations such as this to relax as there always is the anticipation that one day a knock will come on the door saying the body has been found in spite of the time lapse.

I hope Jane's communication so soon after her passing will have helped Lawrence and the rest of the family in knowing that both she and Carl are safe and at peace in spirit, still loving and taking an interest in what is happening to those left behind.

I should like to thank Lawrence and his family for allowing this story to be written and, because the first photo was not very clear, for providing this second one showing Carl with his baby son.

Chapter Thirteen

ANDREW

What I have said about my reason for including particular stories in my books in enabling people to be comforted even though they never visit a medium is true, but obviously it is always difficult to know which to include to help the most.

I have found from the response in letters I receive, that the stories relating to people in spirit, who come through to relate to their family, friends and loved ones, have given many people great comfort and help in understanding what happens to their own special person who has left for the world of spirit, no matter what the way in which they have left. Nowadays, there seems to be a large increase in the numbers of young men leaving through having taken their own lives and I like to include them in each of my books.

This is why I have decided to mention Andrew and dedicate the story to his lovely family who, over the last two years since Andrew left us, have made several visits to talk with him.

I was to have my first contact with Andrew very soon after his passing to the spirit world. Andrew's sisters, Margaret and Sue, were to come for a private sitting. From the very beginning, Andrew made his appearance very positive and loving, confirming that he had taken his own life in the December and, with no hesitation, passed on a considerable amount of information.

For what had been a shy and reserved young man, he certainly showed no signs of "holding back" as he communicated from spirit. He wanted his sisters to know that he was safe and happy now and that he was not alone but had met up with his grandparents. Andrew confirmed that he had only been married for a short while and, while not wanting to say too much about this, did say that their had been some marriage problems and he just could not cope any more. He described his work in the factory and talked about his house, which Margaret and Sue confirmed as being correct, and did not want to miss out on mentioning his Mum and Dad. He mentioned that they had problems with their legs and that Dad had worked on the railways most of his life. He said he was sorry that he had left un-answered questions behind and knew that they were having difficulty coming to terms with his leaving, but hoped that now he was able to communicate, it would help them begin to understand. He mentioned Paul and David, his brothers, and another sister, Julie; he even managed within the sitting to give Margaret and Sue the names of their children and mentioned their characters, not even missing out a mention of Sue's dog called Sam.

Although this young man in his twenties, the babe of the family, was a quiet and sensitive man, he had certainly come into his own now he was in spirit and was obviously happier and more positive. After the sitting finished, Margaret and Sue took the tape intending to let the family hear it.

Andrew

Later on, Andrew's brother, Paul, made a visit and once again Andrew didn't let him down, talking about himself and pulling Paul's leg about his past marriages and discussing Paul's living on his own and working in the factory. Andrew was also aware of Paul's interest in spiritualism and said that, if Paul wanted to, he could develop spiritually and channel his energies into healing, which Paul said he had already started doing. Once one person has been and found the mediumship to be genuine and helpful, those they tell often want to come and have a sitting for themselves, but I never know who they are or how they connect with one another as I only take first names of prospective sitters, and it is not until I know who the communicator is that I realise the connection. It was therefore a nice surprise when I discovered that Paul had told his Mum and Dad about his visit and they decided that not only Margaret, Sue and Paul should have the experience, but that they would come for a sitting too.

I hope that Andrew's family have benefited from their visits to talk with Andrew. I think they must have done because, whenever I have done a demonstration in Andrew's local town, his Mum and Dad and sisters have visited the meetings and I do remember one occasion when Andrew gave them a further message, still showing them all that he is always aware of them and is determined to reassure them that he is happy and at peace in his new home in spirit.

Since the bond with Andrew has been established since his passing in December 1994, it was also a very pleasant surprise when I gave a recent sitting to his other sister who, although living a distance away, had decided to come for herself. Once again, Andrew did not disappoint her and was soon in his stride, telling about her husband, their house and their son, Ben and what he knew about their lives now.

Therefore, I hope that this story of Andrew will show that, even though he was quite a sensitive man and because his passing was not what we would call "natural", he is now really positive, wanting to reassure everybody of his new life. As each and every one of his family came to communicate with him, they all got his individual attention and would know that he still remains their son, brother and uncle and that, whenever they speak of him or include him in their thoughts and prayers, he is there listening and sending back his love.

This particular story, however, has an extra postscript. During December 1996, I stood in for a medium who had had to cancel a demonstration at my local church and I was therefore not listed as the speaker. Nonetheless, Andrew's brother, Paul, was in the congregation and received the first message which came through that evening. I had not seen any of Andrew's family for a few months and, when I began, Andrew told Paul that he had now got his father with him in spirit and that, as his Dad had only been with him for a short while, Andrew wanted the family to know that he was O.K, saying that, although his Dad had found it difficult to accept spiritual communication whilst he was on earth, he himself now wanted to communicate and send his love and thoughts to Ruby, his wife, and to the rest of the family.

He had left suddenly in spite of having been ill with cancer for some time, and commented that he had left as he had wanted to "with his shoes on" due to a heart attack.

People who know me get used to the fact that I have friends who talk to me face to face on the earth-plane and friends who talk to me from the spirit world, but as this story shows, sometimes the same person can speak to me at different points of time from both.

A Brother's Love

I always remember
that cold day in December
As I sat on my own
I answered the 'phone
and was told the tragic news
You had taken your last walk
Oh I cried wishing instead
You'd come to me for a talk
When I imagine the pain you had
I still feel so sad
How much you were hurting inside
I will never know
And still it's so hard to accept
that you decided to go
Often when thinking of you
I close my eyes for a while
I always can picture
your wonderful smile

Least I now know you're at rest
in the place where such a special person
as you deserves the best
You're in heaven looking
down from up above
as I send you all my love
thinking about you every day
missing you more than words can ever say
My feelings for you are so strong
Like your spirit they will always live on
One day you and I will be together
Until then god bless you brother
Now and for ever

Written by Paul for his brother Andrew

Chapter Fourteen

RICHARD (RICH)

The loss of someone we love is always difficult to deal with and at such times, families feel frustrated and unsure where to turn to find help.

In August 1990, a lady telephoned me, saying she had read my book, "Life beyond the Storm" and felt she needed to come for a sitting. She started to tell me about her Mother's passing nine years before, but I stopped her, saying that I would prefer to know nothing in advance of her sitting with me, as I like things to come through naturally from spirit.

As I suggested a date a few weeks' ahead, I instantly became aware of a young voice talking to me, saying that the lady was to come sooner than that. When I said that a young boy was telling me that she was to come sooner and that he had just left us, she became emotional, but as I asked her not to give me any information about it, we agreed that I would see her on the Sunday, which was my day off as it appeared to be both important and urgent. The lady agreed, saying there would be a family of five coming, but didn't want to leave her name in case I associated it consciously with the reason they needed to see me. I said, "O.K., I shall put you in the diary as 'The Family'," and was about to put down the telephone, when I added, "The teenager says he's here with his grandparents and all right".

When the family arrived on the Sunday, they consisted of the lady, her husband and their three sons. Following coffee and a visit to the "loo", we sat down and I started to explain the way I work and what to expect, but had to interrupt to ask a spirit communicator to wait until I had finished explaining, as he was trying to come through at once.

As soon as I had finished my explanation, the young man was able to come through to connect with the family. I informed them that I had with me a young man who in many ways appeared to be older than his years and who never stopped chatting. They all nodded. As I knew only the name of one member of the family by then, that being Mark, the young man proceeded to introduce me to his family. Firstly, he gave me his father's name, which was John, followed by Jonathan, his brother, who apparently also had a nickname. Then turning to another brother who, he said, was married, he named him as Paul and Paul's wife as Jo(anne). Paul's response was understandably emotional when the young man spoke not only of Paul and Joanne's daughter, Kerry, but also of the fact (which he insisted I mention) that there was another baby due soon which he was really looking forward to.

His family confirmed that this information was indeed all correct, and the young man then turned to Mark, his eldest brother. He referred to the fact that Mark had recently split up from his girl-friend, Karen, and reassured Mark that he had been right in putting their house up for sale, adding some personal messages both to Mark and to Karen.

It was then his Mum's turn. I was given a name which sounded like "Sin", and she replied, "Yes. I'm called Cynthia, but he often called me 'Cyn'"; so very quickly, this young man made sure of establishing his strong and lively presence with us, adding that his birthday which was due the following month (September) would still be celebrated even though he was now in spirit.

Once I could get a word in, I asked him for his own name and he answered, "Ricky – Rich – really Richard", which they said was just like him, but that he was usually known as "Rich".

Even having given me his name, Richard seemed determined to continue to talk about his family rather than about how he had left us. He gave me information about the birthdays of his mother and brother Mark and said that he had met up with his two grandfathers in spirit and also his grandma, who were looking after him. He was determined to say everything he wanted to, talking first to one member of the family, then another.

He talked to Paul about his terraced house, especially drawing attention to the front door (which Paul said Rich had helped to paint) and described the bay window there. He told me that Paul worked in a factory and mentioned his moped-type of bike, saying that it was "out the back" as it was no longer used now that Paul was having driving lessons. Rich suggested Paul leave the test until after the baby's arrival, but joked that he had best learn to drive so he could take the children out later on, adding that, if the baby proved to be a boy, he should be given the name "Richard" as a second name, not a first, and the family agreed that this had already been mentioned.

Richard then concentrated on his brother Mark, saying that both Mark and Jonathan worked with food at "Morrison's", which was correct, but added that Jonathan was not keen on his recent job of filling shelves and would soon move on to something different. Rich then asked Mark if he was going to train as a manager which surprised Mark, as only the previous day he had been offered the chance to go on a trainee management course but had felt unsure about this, and Rich enthusiastically encouraged him to do so. Richard then turned his attention to his mother, explaining how she felt and that she had been helped by working with children as a child-minder. Cynthia explained that she had been unable to do this since Richard had left, but, although his mother disagreed, he insisted that she would return to child-minding again later.

At this point, Richard decided to get around to discussing his passing, explaining that it had been an accident and not his intention, as he had been playing and experimenting, never for a moment expecting such an outcome and that he wanted them all to know this, explaining that his passing had been very quick and without pain.

Obviously, this was of some help to his family but, as they said, "It's so very hard to understand 'Why?'".

The young Richard wanted to talk to his family about details of the funeral. He told me that he was "football mad" and showed me a red and white scarf with "Nottingham Forest" on it. He said he was pleased that he was buried in his Forest football kit with the scarf and also a photograph of his family. This apparently was of his Gran and Grandad and his Mum was pleased he knew of this.

Rich decided then to talk to his Dad, John, saying that his Dad was quiet and never said much. He talked about his work and the problems he had with backache (which John confirmed), and Rich told his Dad that he had met Grandad and talked about his Grandma who was still on earth and of Gran's Irish background. He added to his Mum that his Aunty Margaret whom he had never known was also with him and helping him, even though she had passed a long time before with cancer.

When he insisted that I talk about his freckles and ginger hair, his Mum confirmed that he had always fretted and worried about them. The whole time he was talking to me, I felt that he was doing Judo or Karate-chops at someone, and Mark confirmed that this was just what Rich was always doing, in fun, to him. It was obviously an emotional moment for Mark who, of all the family, seemed least able to come to terms with Richard's unexpected passing.

It made everyone smile, however, when Rich started taking the mickey about someone's chipped teeth, as Paul answered that his young brother had always pulled his leg about his chipped teeth. Rich then mentioned that his brother Jonathan would be starting to learn to drive following his next birthday when he would be seventeen and joked about Jonathan's girl-friend, saying that he would be watching to see what he got up to now, and added that Paul would be 24 the following February.

The family were surprised then, as Richard went on to mention aunts, uncles and cousins – a lot on his Mum's side, but not many on Dad's – listing, Uncle George, Aunty Rose, Uncles Albert, Brian, Tommy and Kenny, Aunty Pam, Bett, Jan, and his cousins Nigel, Thomas, Michelle, Sue and many others, much to their astonishment, although they had all been at the funeral and obviously Rich was aware of this.

The young lad then mentioned his rabbit which the family had always looked after in the past, since he never did and which his Mum and Dad had threatened to give away, but which was still there. He mentioned his dislike for school, saying he had only gone because he had to and would much rather have been with his family as school was not important to him.

Richard appeared to me to be a very lively, caring boy indeed, who at the age of thirteen had everything to live for but, sadly for his family, had lived out his life-span on earth and been called to the world of spirit.

In those short years, he had nonetheless made his mark on friends and family alike. Rich will continue to be aware of them and able to offer help from spirit on occasion, watching the changes which take place within the family circle and knowing that he is still in their hearts.

Although this thirteen-year-old boy had been in spirit for only three weeks when all this happened, he was able to come and to unite with his family, giving them the assurance that from his new vantage point in spirit with family members there, he was still part of his earth family, watching and listening to them and letting them know that "Rich" is just a touch away.

Chapter Fifteen

STEVE (SKET)

In September 1989 I received a call from a lady named Jackie who was feeling very low at the time. She had been advised to contact me to see if I could help her come to terms with a recent passing. She had just lost her husband, Steve in a mini-coach accident, at the age of thirty-five, and wanted confirmation that what she was doing was in accord with Steve's wishes.

At this stage, I was able to link up with Steve in the spirit world. He confirmed that he had left instantly at the time of the accident but was very concerned about another member of the coach party who was in a coma in hospital. He said that the person would be all right and that he was being helped from spirit to carry on.

Steve continued by giving Jackie information about her mother, Flo, in spirit and about his father. He expressed concern regarding his children and gave their names as Ricky and Michelle. Jackie confirmed that the names were correct, and Steve went on to say how pleased he was to feel closer to his family than before, as there had been problems with the marriage in the past; he was content with the funeral arrangements and wanted his ashes scattered on Tottenham Football Club ground which was what Jackie was having carried out. Steve continued by giving Jackie names and birthday dates of friends and family and, as the messages came to a close, she asked me if a proper sitting could be arranged with Steve's Mum (Elsie) and his friend, Darren, and a date was made for a few weeks later.

When Jackie, Elsie and Darren arrived at my home, they decided all to sit together and Jackie asked permission to tape the sitting. I agreed, and Steve came through very strongly, giving his nick-name, "Sket", which I kept pronouncing wrongly, frequently calling him "Skeet" by mistake!

Sket talked about the last moments of his life here on earth and said that people had been talking about whether he and his friends had been drinking prior to the accident. Sket said that, although they had had some beers, he did not feel this caused the accident as he had not had enough to lose control. For some strange reason, they had made the journey many times but that day they had taken a wrong turning and so had not stopped, as they usually did, for fish and chips, and had continued cheerfully and noisily on their way home along the road which was more winding and narrow than their usual route.

Sket wanted to talk about how the mini-coach swerved and hit another car saying that, until the moment of the accident, he had been in control of the vehicle.

Having got all this off his chest, Sket continued to talk generally about his family and friends, giving advice to Darren and talking about his funeral. He said that he liked the wreath in the shape of a pillow from his children, Michelle and Ricky (who was also known as "Sket"). This was confirmed by Jackie as being correct. Sket was very insistent about a red and white wreath which he said was special and Jackie mistakenly thought he was referring to a wreath which was half Tottenham Hotspur colours and half Nottingham Forest, until she returned home. At home she played her tape and looked at photographs of the wreaths, and then realised that her husband had been talking about the heart-shaped white wreath with a single red rose in it, which she had herself sent.

Sket had continued the sitting by laughing about the fact that he didn't have to pay to watch Tottenham play any more, as now it was free to him and he wouldn't be missing any matches now he was himself part of the ground. Although Sket talked to Jackie for most of the sitting, part of the time was taken up by his father and mother-in-law who also came through and confirmed that they had all met up.

Sket expressed concern about his fellow team members, particularly those who were still very ill in hospital, but he said he would try to help with their improvement, however slow it might be. Jackie, Elsie and Darren were reassured and comforted by their contact with Sket and said they could accept what had come through. Some months later, I had another request for a sitting from Jackie, asking if she and Elsie could bring Sket's children with them, as they had listened to the tape and wanted to come to talk to their father. This sitting took place in April 1990.

First of all, Jackie came in to see me alone, as she wanted to see if Sket had been listening to what she had been saying to him, and needed some guidance. At first, it was Jackie's Mum who came through, saying that when Sket had arrived in spirit, she had given him a ticking off (Sket's version was a little stronger than this!) but that all was O.K. now. Jackie's mother was concerned about her husband's health, saying that it was not very good, and Jackie confirmed that this was so. After her Mum had passed on a few more messages, Sket came through to talk to Jackie. He knew she was still having difficulty coming to terms with his passing and said he knew she was considering attending evening classes for typewriting which he thought was a good idea, as when the children were older she might be able to make a career for herself and she said she had already been making enquiries about this the week before. Sket told Jackie that after a while she would move house and that she was not helping herself by putting emphasis on material things and memories of Sket in the house, saying that eventually she would have strength to make these moves. She confirmed that other personal messages I passed on to her were correct and I asked whether there was anything else she wished to ask Sket. She took a sheet of paper from her handbag, checked it, and answered, "No. Sket has definitely been listening to me". She said that he had answered all of her questions without her telling me, and that she was aware that Sket's presence was around her and that he was helping her.

It was now time for Elsie, Sket's mother, and his children, Michelle and Ricky, to come into the room. Once they had settled down and I had explained to them about their father in spirit, Sket wanted to say that he wanted to wish Michelle a happy tenth birthday the following month. This was correct and it made Michelle happy. Sket continued to talk to his daughter about her schoolwork, saying he had been watching her swimming and was very impressed with her progress. It was then the turn of Ricky to have his Dad talk to him about the trophy he had got at football and about the fact that Sket had been watching Ricky's progress as goalkeeper. Sket then went on to talk about the fact that he agreed with Jackie that Ricky should wait until he was a bit older before having his ear pierced as he wanted, and Ricky said, "O.K". Sket corrected Ricky for some bad language he had acquired and mentioned the fact that his B.M.X. bike was out of action because it had been smashed and put in the shed. Ricky confirmed that this was true. Ricky was pleased that his Dad wished him a happy ninth birthday in November the day before Bonfire Night and that his Dad remarked on the Tottenham Hotspur kit he was wearing.

After chatting to his children a while longer, Sket spoke to his mother, Elsie, saying he knew that she had not been well recently due to a slight chest condition, but reassured that this would soon be better. He told her that he liked her new three piece suite and that he and his Dad (who was in spirit with him) agreed about the new carpet she was having, his father leaving him to do all the talking and keeping quiet as he had when he had been here on earth.

Sket then started to talk about the holiday that Jackie, Elsie and the children were going to have down in Devon. Jackie said that this was correct; they were going away to Torquay. Sket said he would be with them.

Once Sket had said all he had been wanting to say and sending them all his love, the children wanted to ask questions. They both wanted to know if their Dad looked like he did when he left or whether he was younger now. Sket laughed and said he would stay the same as they knew him, although he would still have his birthdays and get older, but spiritually, not physically, which his children surprisingly seemed to understand. Ricky asked if his Dad would be surfing with him on his holiday at the coast and Sket said he would so long as Ricky left room for him on the back of the surf-board, which made Ricky laugh. While Michelle had been sitting out in the other room, she had written a poem about my cats which she gave me and I felt this should be included in the book.

To bryn

Cats

Cats can be all sorts of colours black and white and giger too they purr so sweetly when they are asleep there so sweet and furry and cuddly you shouldent pull their tail you should love them comEet them and look after them propley and they will love you Just like you love them.

From michelle
Skets dauther

Poem from Sket's daughter, Michelle

So, you see, even children love to be able to have the chance to talk with their loved ones in spirit. Children should not be kept "in the dark" about death. It is important to try to explain to them where their loved ones have gone, knowing that they still love and care for them.

Children, more often than not, have the courage and simplicity to ask straightforward questions about just the things that we want to know and are too afraid to ask.

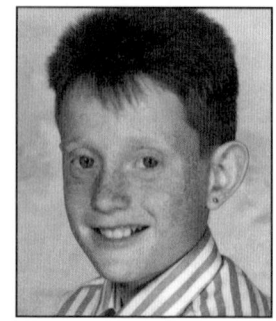

Paul *Steve (Sket)* *Richard*

MESSAGES FROM THE GRAVE

An interview with Steve's wife Jackie

Messages from a dead man have changed the life of a Grantham widow who turned to spiritualism after her husband was killed in a tragic minibus crash. Jackie McGettigan of Redmile Walk, has sought comfort from medium Bryan Gibson in a bid to understand her experiences.

Her husband Steve was killed in the crash in September 1989, which left his pub football team mates injured and ended the life of a car driver. And now the man who tunes in to messages from beyond the grave has revealed how he has helped many families come to terms with their grief.

Jackie and her two children, Michelle (11) and Ricky (9), have experienced many attempts at communication with Steve, she said. They have smelled his aftershave, seen shadows in the house, heard a tapping sound (Steve "had this habit of tapping his ring"), and noticed his football trophies have been moved while the family were out.

"There are people who say it's a load of rubbish, but that's because they don't want to believe and they are scared about it," said Jackie.

"So people have got mixed feelings about it. Until my husband was killed I was borderline in my beliefs."

Jackie now sends other people to Mr. Gibson for help and has started visiting a spiritualist church in Sleaford.

"It's changed my life for the better. Without it I would still be grieving quite a lot," she said.

Jackie added that Mr. Gibson has passed on messages from Steve - "personal information" that he could never have known about, she said. The facts that he gave me were marvellous."

From the *Grantham Journal*

Chapter Sixteen

PAUL

A great many people pass through my life as they try to connect with their loved ones who have left the earth-plane. Some of those people become particularly important and, although I never knew their loved ones when they were on the earth, they themselves become special friends of mine in the spirit world. One of these special friends of mine is called Paul.

Paul left us on November 19th 1989 as the result of an accident, at the age of eighteen. At the beginning of 1990, Paul's mother, Lucy, came to see me with Paul's sister, Sam, and his brother, Daniel, with their stepfather, Dave.

At first, the sitting was very emotional, but Paul was able to chat to his family about his work in the building trade, saying that he lived with his grandmother in Brighton. He gave off the month of his passing and mentioned family birthdays. He told his family how he had met up with Shaun, a friend of his in spirit who had also left at an early age and spoke about his natural father, Bill, who was in spirit. He talked to Dave whom he regarded as his Dad and his friend, about his lorry driving and how he had gone with him in the past on his trips, especially referring to the music of Rod Stewart which he always played. Paul mentioned that Dave had a hearing problem in one ear, but I felt that – apart from this – Dave was having a real problem accepting what was going on. Paul talked to his young brother, Daniel, saying he hoped that Daniel would stick at his college work and talked to Sam about the work she was now doing in an office instead of her earlier hairdressing. Paul spoke about his four half-brothers and half-sister and named them, and the sitting was recorded as he chatted about many incidents relating to his family and friends.

Throughout the discussion which followed the sitting about spiritual things and about how I saw Paul, I was aware of doubting that Dave could believe what he had heard. When Lucy telephoned a few days later to thank me for the sitting, she said that Dave had taken a few days before he was able to talk about it at all, but that although he now agreed that the information given was correct, he still could not believe that it was all what it seemed to be, and was still trying to find a logical explanation.

In August 1990, the family booked to visit me again. On this occasion, Paul's brother – Daniel – couldn't make it, but Paul's Grandma who had travelled up with Sam, came instead. Again the sitting was recorded and, as it began, Paul started to sing "Happy Birthday", saying it was for Daniel whose 17th birthday was that week and that he would now want to learn to drive. Turning to Sam, he wished her a happy birthday for July, saying that the next year would be her 21st. With Sam, he discussed her office work and the different computers she used, her boyfriend who had connections with Yorkshire, and mentioned some of his and Sam's joint friends on earth and his friend, Shaun, who was in spirit with him.

In talking to his Mum, Paul said that he had had his 19th birthday in June, the same month as Lucy's. He commented that she was now thinking about getting part-time work such as in being a care assistant and Lucy agreed that this was right. Paul talked about his half-brothers and sister, mentioning that Mark was in a cadet uniform and would have connections with Scotland and it emerged that was something being planned for the following year.

Paul's stepdad, Dave, was a little more relaxed than before, and Paul discussed his change of work, saying that he was driving less now and was using a fork-lift now to load with. Dave agreed and also confirmed Paul was right in saying that he was having trouble with his teeth (for the first time in twenty years) and had recently been to hospital.

Paul's Grandmother had been having difficulty in coming to terms with losing him, and he talked with her about this and about his room at her home which was still the same as when he had been there. He also told her that he had been at his Uncle Shaun's wedding in April and made her laugh by saying that he was keeping an eye on her in her part-time shop work and the number of sweets she ate during the day.

Paul talked to his family about how his half-brother had got a black eye at school and how Daniel had recently changed the lock on the mobile home he lived in alongside the main house to stop the others getting in. He also told them that he had now got the sunglasses he had always wanted. At one stage, Paul asked about a tape which made Dave smile, as Dave had been meant to set the video to record the Grand Prix and had forgotten; this being a very up-to-date incident, it showed Paul's current awareness of what his family were doing.

I was a little confused about a silver-plated article which Paul showed me, but Lucy replied that she had just bought a silverplated rose bowl for Paul's 19th birthday with a card and had put them beside Paul's picture with flowers in the bowl, and she was pleased to realise that Paul knew of both his present and card.

He also mentioned his half-brother's athletic ability and the certificate he had recently gained for it and his young sister Amanda and her musical ability, which made everyone laugh.

As the sitting came to an end, Sam said she had been hoping to hear more from Shaun, but Paul commented that today was his day and he had wanted to come to talk, especially as his Grandma was there and he had wanted to give all the messages himself. In sending his love to all of them, he added that he knew it would be a traumatic time when the November anniversary of his passing came around, but that he would be with them, sending his love and thoughts out to them.

Following the sitting, Paul's Mum gave me a copy of the poem she had felt inspired to write and it is enclosed here for everyone to read, as Lucy hopes that it will also help others who have lost someone dear to them.

As you will realise, Paul and his family have themselves become an extension of my numerous friends both in spirit and on earth.

I hope that for many years to come I may have the honour to link with Paul and his family, giving his love, help, guidance and laughter, helping them all to remember that he will always be just a touch away from them.

A TRIBUTE

"This little poem I have written shows the hope, the joy and the love that you have given me. I do hope that you can use it, perhaps to let other parents see that nothing is lost and nothing changes. Love remains the same. At 5.30 am one morning, I felt I needed to write down exactly how I felt and I even surprised myself!

Much love and more besides goes to you for Love and Joy you gave to us in our darkest moments.

Thankyou once again.

Lucy, Dave, Sam and Daniel."

PAUL

I still have a son who's close to me
One I can talk with, but cannot see.
He's there beside me in all I do,
In darker days, he helps me through.

I miss his laughter and long to touch
That first-born son that I love so much.
I know I'm luckier than most parents have been
For when he passed over he was just eighteen.

Those happy years I treasure with joy.
I know, I still have my oldest boy.
I don't despair for all is not gone.
I just hold out my hand and he follows along.

For I was chosen by the spirits above
A special mother, to receive special love.
Our bond is not broken; It still stays the same,
I still have my son and Paul is his name.

Chapter Seventeen

A TRIBUTE TO VI

August 1988 was the time when a close, dear friend of mine named Vi had to leave us for the spirit world, having suffered from cancer during the previous few years. This very special lady had come into my life in July 1963 when we became neighbours in Bexley, Kent. She became like a second "Mum" to me and we remained close friends even after Vi moved to Cliftonville and I moved on in a different direction. We always stayed close friends, no matter how many miles separated us, even when I eventually left the South for my new life in Lincolnshire. Vi took in her stride my newly acquired spiritual awareness and change of lifestyle although, at the time, she admitted that she did not believe in the reality of an after-life.

Vi continued to live a normal life following her cancer operation, accepting her illness and determining to make the most of her children and grandchildren.

The end of Vi's life was gradually approaching after many months of hospital treatment, when I visited her in May 1988. We spent some very special moments reminiscing about the 25 years we had known each other, recalling the ups and downs of those years and it was a very moving time which will always stay in my heart.

Together we talked openly about death and life after, of how people in the spirit world united and linked together, particularly mentioning Charlie, Vi's husband, who had left for the spirit world following a very sudden heart attack. During my short stay, I gave Vi healing which helped her relax and eased some of the discomfort she was then experiencing at that time.

About two months later, Vi's condition deteriorated much sooner than had been anticipated and she required frequent attention and treatment. Just a week before Vi passed peacefully into the world of spirit, I had the urge to telephone to see how she was, and her sister, who answered, told me that she was very tired and unable to come to the phone. Vi's sister told me that they had been discussing my spiritual gift and had been looking together at the cuttings which I had recently sent her about the work I was now doing. As the conversation with Vi's sister relaxed and became a little lighter, I was suddenly made aware of a photograph of Vi in front of me; in the photo she had a cigarette in one hand and a parrot on the other. We both laughed about this because the parrot was a family joke. Charlie and Vi had this parrot when I first met them and it was quite awesome. It had the habit of dive-bombing you whenever you entered the room and it was not too fond of men, so often it was Charlie who ended up running for cover. The parrot was quite a character and it often escaped and landed in the oak tree opposite, with us in hot pursuit climbing a ladder to catch him in a net before he came to harm. Sadly, he eventually had to go and moved house to a happy home with another parrot, but it took quite a while for me to be able to visit Vi's house without looking upwards in anticipation of the swish of wings as I entered. However, singling out that particular memory at the time seemed a little strange, as it had all happened more than twenty years previously.

Vi and her parrot

A week later, I was told of Vi's passing into the spirit world. Being by now very heavily committed with sittings at home and church bookings, I was concerned at not being able to attend the funeral. I checked my diary and was sorry to see I had only one day free and that was ten days ahead, with no possible time at which I could attend earlier when the ceremony was anticipated. Imagine my surprise when David, Vi's son, 'phoned me to tell me the date of the funeral – yes, it was on the one day which had been kept free for months. I felt that spirit must have taken into account even that long before the event, how upset and frustrated I should have been to have had to miss saying "Goodbye" to this very special, brave lady who was more like part of my family than a friend.

On my arrival at David's home for the funeral, one of the first things I was given was a black and white photograph of Vi – yes, with a cigarette in one hand and the parrot on the other – exactly as I had described it over the telephone to Vi's sister. I had never before seen that photograph in my life, and to me it felt that Vi wanted me to have this very special remembrance of our friendship. It now has a special place in my home along with the many other photographs given to me by the many people with whom I have had communication from the world of spirit.

The day of Vi's funeral was not a sad day for us, but a special day of peace and love joined with laughter as we recalled the memories we all shared of this remarkable lady. The remainder of the day and evening slipped by as Vi's family and friends and I discussed spirit communication and the world to which she had gone.

We all felt that Vi was in the room with us, laughing and enjoying a drink as she would always have done, but we also knew that she was at peace and had met up with Charlie, her husband.

Losing someone dear to us is always sad, but it gives us great happiness to know that they are at peace and continue to be just as much part of their family here on earth as they ever were.

Chapter Eighteen

DEMONSTRATIONS

There is quite a difference between those personal sittings conducted in private on a one-to-one basis and the material which is communicated in public demonstrations to large gatherings and audiences such as in theatres. Privacy enables some of the best communication to come through to sitters, as in other situations detail has to be limited – mostly to the names of those in spirit and special shared memories and dates of anniversaries for instance, as I do not like to pass on anything too personal or embarrassing from the platform and tend to ask people to see me afterwards about such details. Also, some communicators tend to be very insistent and need control, as otherwise few people would get a look in as far as receiving messages is concerned, which would be very boring for the audience. It is very frustrating for a medium to bring through information from spirit which is correct in a public demonstration, to be told by the recipient that they do not understand the message and to have that person come up afterwards to say, "Sorry. I was embarrassed by that message. It was correct, but I didn't want to admit it because of what other people would think".

It is better to provide such information privately. I feel that if I have been given a message to pass on, then it should be something which is understood by the recipient and I do not like to leave half-understood messages with people for them to think about later.

It is not always easy to be clear about such things. Sometimes I have been faced with a situation in which a number of people in the audience have claimed to relate to all the names and information in a particular spirit communication. At one demonstration at the seaside, three ladies were sitting near one another, two together and one in the row in front of them. Every name, each anniversary and relationship I mentioned was claimed by each of them, but, with the supportive laughter and encouragement of the audience, I eventually managed to sort out the lady the message really was intended for, and to deliver the intended communication.

Demonstrations can be as different as chalk from cheese. It must be every medium's nightmare to fear "getting nothing" at a demonstration, but we cannot

*A charity demonstration at Woolsthorpe village hall,
to raise money for a hospital unit in Leicester*

afford to show "butterflies in the stomach" even when we feel them! On the other hand, there are nights when spirit vibrations are very powerful indeed and you feel everything is sure to go right.

One such night began hesitantly, but we soon got in our stride and someone was happily accepting the message when an extra boost of energy flowed through me. I felt a very strong lady come through and announce to the gathering that she knew them all there and wanted to say "Hello". She gave her name and the man receiving the message said, "That's my wife and she belonged to this church".

The lady went on to talk to them about another member of the church who was seriously ill in hospital and said that she had that afternoon gone with her husband to visit the hospital, and this was confirmed as correct. She told them that she was sending healing to help him regain strength, and the emotion of those present was obvious in relating to this message, as the lady herself had been in spirit only about a year. She humourously pulled her husband's leg about his increased weight and joked about his Scottish ancestry, relaxing everyone and passing on messages to her friends, thanking them for the lovely flowers they had placed in the church when she passed to the spirit world. The evening just seemed to flow by in this spiritual atmosphere and, when the time came for the last message, it was directed to three ladies who were sitting together right at the very back of the church.

Demonstrating with Coral Polge at The Lawns, Lincoln, April 1997

The spirit gentleman who was talking to me gave me the name of either "Michael" or "Michelle" and the youngest lady said, "That's me". I told her that her Grandfather was with me and wanted her to know that he was all right and that he was very pleased and proud of her and the training she was doing. (Apparently, her Grandfather had wanted her to teach, and she had just completed her first year's teaching.) He talked to her about a photograph which she had just framed and she agreed that she had just framed a photo of her brother. He wanted her to move it as it was in a dark place and he wanted it to be nearer the window, and she agreed.

It then became apparent that all three ladies were related, as the gentleman, who gave his name as "Bill", started to talk to his wife. He told her he was pleased that she was going to move and had already "packed his bags" to go with her, which produced some amazed gasps as this was so up-to-date as this had only come about that week. The lady responded that she was really pleased with this information, as she had been unsure about the move and felt she would now be able to settle in the new home.

He then turned his attention to the lady in the middle, who proved to be his daughter, talking to her about her worries about the safety of her son who worked in the Fire Brigade, and saying he would keep an eye on him to make sure he was O.K. Just as he was finishing speaking to her, he said to me, "Say the name Joan to her", which I did – and the lady replied, "That is me". So Bill – their husband, father and grandfather – had given them all positive evidence of his survival in spirit.

When I was talking to the three, very emotional ladies following the service, I found that that day was the third anniversary of his going to the spirit world, so it was very special to them.

It is really a pleasure to get such confirmation of the help which can be provided through the work which we do, enabling people to come to terms with the loss of loved ones, knowing that, when our life here on earth is completed, we and our loved ones will all be united again. We can truly look forward to that life with those in spirit who are even now "just a touch away".

Chapter Nineteen

COMMUNICATION FROM SPIRIT

I suppose that, nowadays, nothing should surprise me, but even I am amazed sometimes by the determination of some spirit communicators to get a message through even in situations where the person receiving the sitting is neither related nor connected to them personally.

Recently, halfway through a sitting in which I was passing on messages about someone's family and friends, I became aware of a beautiful little girl in the spirit world. She was making me aware of her presence with her truly lovely smile and her beautiful eyes. Since I did not feel she belonged to the sitter, I asked her for some information, and she told me that she had had Down's Syndrome and had passed to the world of spirit when she was in hospital a few months earlier.

I told my sitter, asking if the information meant anything to her. She was obviously taken aback and appeared emotionally affected by this, saying, "Yes. A young couple who live in the same village as me, lost a little girl at the beginning of the year." She had gone into hospital to have one of whole series of operations, but had died suddenly before the operation, and the sitter said that she often used to talk to the child's mother. The little girl then started to deliver a message for her mother, saying that she was fine now and at peace, saying she could now talk, and mentioned her older sister here on earth who was now doing all right. My sitter promised that she would pass on the child's message next time she saw the mother, and the little girl smiled, and left us.

Returning to the sitter to pass on messages from her family, we approached the end of the sitting. Once more I was aware of the lovely child reappearing and saying that her mother's name had been given to the sitter to show who she was. On asking the sitter whether this was correct, she replied after a little thought, "Of course. You mention the name 'Jane', but I only thought of my cousin Jane. I would not have associated it with the little girl if you hadn't said that, as it's a while now since she left and I wouldn't have associated the name with her mother."

Once more, a spirit message had been relayed from a spirit communicator who wanted to get a connection with their family, in the hope that even such an indirect link would enable them to know that they are just a touch away from those who love them. That situation reminds me about a young lady whom I saw urgently. The urgent booking was made as a result of a telephone call from the girl's mother.

The boyfriend of the girl's closest friend had been for a sitting with me and apparently it had been like a game of "Chinese Whispers". A message originating with spirit had been passed through me to the boyfriend to the effect that the young lady in question would not now be doing something she had earlier planned to do. He had told his girlfriend about this but felt it should not be passed on; the girlfriend passed it on nonetheless to the young lady, who decided that it must mean that she would be unable to go to Australia as she planned two months ahead. She was very worried and imagined all sorts of dire reasons for this, and her mother sensibly decided to check with me about what the message actually meant.

The young lady herself had been told through me at an earlier sitting that she would travel to Australia as she was planning, and this had been confirmed to her mother at a subsequent sitting at mine. However, I was asked, did the new message relate to the trip to Australia and was that what I had said? As I held the telephone receiver in my hand, I asked guidance from spirit, which I immediately received.

I was told that something the girl had planned she would not now be doing, but that the message had been misinterpreted. Someone did not wish her to go and wished that they were going either with her or instead of her. I was impressed to ask whether the girlfriend had been asked not to speak to her of this matter but had gone ahead and done so anyway, which proved to be the case. However, to make certain that the girl did not continue to feel afraid, I arranged to see her the following week.

When she arrived, I again linked up with spirit. It was confirmed that, since her last visit, her life had changed due to the breakdown of her relationship and the coming trip to Australia had become very important to her. It was confirmed that she would indeed go there, even specifying the name of Melbourne which surprised her, as that was her destination.

Spirit continued to give her positive thoughts and reasons for the apparent confusion, drawing attention to her friend's not wanting her to go. She confirmed that this was how her friend felt and, once spirit had answered all her questions, she said she was once again looking forward without fear to her adventure.

I draw attention to this event so that you understand how important it is to make sure any message passed on via someone else is properly understood and clarified if it is not straightforward. Always check with the medium if you do not understand and make sure you do not present a message in a way which will upset someone or make them afraid, as this is not what spirit wishes. Spiritual messages are intended for help, guidance and love, never to hurt, hinder or distress people, but we have freedom of choice as to how we use the information which they provide. Let us make sure that we do so responsibly.

Spirit obviously trusted that young lady as a reliable link, as she herself was used in a special way to convey a message.

A young man, in his early twenties, who had left through an accident, made himself known to me and the young woman confirmed that she knew who he was. He explained that he had worked for the railway and had fallen from electric cables; he told me that he had lived in Sydney and the sitter was his sister's friend. The young man asked her to let his family know that he was all right, telling her that he had not suffered and had passed quickly to spirit. He left us smiling, knowing that he had bridged the gap between the physical and spirit planes, arranging for his message to be delivered even from the other side of the world.

Chapter Twenty

DIFFERENT PEOPLE – DIFFERENT LIVES

One of the joys of being a medium is that you come into contact with many different kinds of people.

Mediums are visited for widely differing reasons. Some folk are desperate for reassurance about their loved ones' existence in the world of spirit. Some come for what they hope will be sound advice and guidance about their lives. A few come out of curiosity because their friends or family have been and they wish to see and hear for themselves and come to a conclusion about what they think is happening, and the reactions of the various people differ according to their reasons for coming.

As a medium, I try not to categorise people in any way when I meet them because what they really are on the inside may be very different from what they appear to be on first meeting them, and it is so rewarding to be able to find out who the inner person is and enjoy who they really are, or can be.

All of us tend to be "programmed" by what we have been told as children. The images offered to us by our parents, grandparents, teachers or whatever are very powerful, and we sometimes grow up thinking that people such as "Mr or Mrs so-and-so" are people we should avoid or imitate because we are told to do so. It is obviously useful to have guidelines as we grow up but we need to remember that these are just other people's ideas and we need to form our own, taking the trouble to get to know and understand first-hand what people are like and not just being prejudiced; otherwise we may judge people completely wrongly. It wasn't until I became spiritually aware that I understood the difference and now, when people come to see me, I am interested in the person inside, not how they speak or how they dress. But, whatever they may be like, it is not my job to try to change them; I am just the passer-on of messages from the spirit world to them.

Having worked with people with a wide range of lifestyles, backgrounds and differing work connections, I know how important it is to treat everyone as an individual. Also, the very nature of the work means that I am in the privileged position of being privy to all sorts of personal information and, for the duration of a sitting, am taken into the confidence of family communicators as they discuss personal matters which concern them. It is important to realise that, as soon as the sitting has ended, so has your connection with the information. I do not retain it in any way or use it to gossip to other people. It remains strictly private.

It is very sad when mediums are heard giving off information to the media about their sittings with famous people. Obviously this is O.K. if they have the permission of the person concerned to divulge such information, but mostly what we are watching is an ego-centred medium wanting publicity for themselves and their work.

Whether it is a celebrity or an ordinary person like myself, I always ask permission to use material relating to sitters, sending copies of stories to the person or family concerned to make sure they are acceptable and accurate, since, unless they are written shortly after a sitting, words get changed and the whole feeling of the incident can be lost.

So we see that a three-way situation exists:- the spirit communicator, the person receiving the message, and the medium and they must all be in harmony for the communication to work well.

The stories used, as in this book, hopefully can help others – perhaps in similar situations – who may not have the courage to visit a medium but are prepared to read such a book and can develop understanding of what it is possible to achieve.

I know this happens because of the people who have contacted me, never having met me, to say my book was passed to them by a friend, and it has helped and some want to know more.

Obviously books only sell or get recommended by others according to their value and mine are written in the hope of helping increase people's understanding, not just so that I can be a "big-head" and say, "Oh, I have written a book!". The experiences and stories about the work are offered for this reason, in the hope that the heartfelt and humourous anecdotes will also reach through the blocks in people's minds and hearts and make a difference to their lives.

The wide range of people requesting sittings and coming to the demonstrations include many from abroad who keep in touch and suggest that friends visiting this country contact me during their time here. Members of the police force, forces personnel, doctors and clergy as well as Mormons and Jehovah's Witnesses have been known to pay a visit, and request a sitting. Unlike many people, these particular men and women have proved open-minded and feel they cannot judge what goes on until they have seen for themselves. As far as theatre and television are concerned, I have worked with people from both. Although we have been taught to revere them as "idols", they are no different from us in reality. Celebrities, like everyone else, should be treated with respect – but as a person in their own right, not as the image they portray in the media.

This is leading up to why I decided to include this particular chapter in my book. Today I had a return visit from a young lady who came for a sitting four years ago and made a very big impression on me. She is a very attractive long-haired blonde, very petite, with an enormous personality.

On her first visit, I was able to focus on a little of her lifestyle which her grandparents wished to discuss and say how very proud they were of her. Yes, our "Sam" is a Sun page 3 girl and her grandparents confirmed that they were proudly watching her career.

It was interesting how this particular Sam came to visit me. She had been recommended to call by her friend, also called Sam, who had visited me a few weeks previously and who was also a "Page 3 girl" but who herself lived in Lincoln, so I saw two Page 3 lovelies within weeks!

Sam (from Worksop) came back to see me, mainly to bring a relative who had recently lost a little boy with cancer and, knowing my work, wanted to provide this Mum with a link with her son, which I found lovely and very moving. Since Sam also sat throughout the sitting with the little boy's mother, she herself had her leg pulled by the little boy, Shaun, and also received communication from her grandparents about the positive changes in her life and saying that, as well as modelling, she was now looking forward to starting her own family.

At the end of the sitting, I asked Sam if she would allow me to mention her in the book and possibly have a photo to go with the story, and she kindly agreed. Since I am writing this the same day, Sam has promised to post the latest one which I thought would make the book a little more interesting and hope no one will be offended with the photo of such a lovely, special lady.

In Sam's everyday life, she does not go out of her way to get attention and looks like many of the young ladies who come for sittings but, when you talk to her, she "lights up" and the inner glow shines through and makes her stand out in a crowd. I am very grateful to Sam for allowing me to "show off" about my link with her as one of the many different and special people that I have had the honour and privilege to know and to work with. Thanks, Sam!

Another sitting involved a very well-known person who is still in the news even though he has been in spirit for some considerable time now.

It came about because I was invited to go to London to stay with someone starring in the show "Phantom of the Opera" who had been for a sitting in my home. Some of his "show-biz" friends who had heard his taped sitting requested that he invite me down, and so it was arranged that I stay at his home to spend three days giving private sittings to a mixture of people. Some were from "Phantom of the Opera", some were from T.V. and the media and others from the theatre world.

One couple who sat together who had been in show business but were now living in Malta, recorded their very lively sitting. They were able to receive communication not only from their family, but also from many fellow artists who had gone to spirit. Because this sitting was so very full of energy and love,

Sam Tomlinson, model and Page 3 girl
Photo by Jim Carter

I was suddenly stopped in mid-stream; my whole attitude and communication seemed to change drastically. I turned to the lady and said, "Robert wishes to say 'Hello' to you. He was known as 'Bob'." That was it. No more information was forwarded. The lady said she knew exactly who he was and wasn't a bit surprised that he wouldn't say any more. Once again the sitting reverted to its lively humour and confirmed information. When the recorder had been stopped, the lady said to me, "I'll tell you who Bob is now. He is my Uncle Bob – better known as Robert Maxwell. Now you can guess why he kept quiet!"

Another very unexpected communicator linked with me when a retired vicar started to visit me. He had come all the way from Brandon in Suffolk by train and taxi.

Now this is one sitting which, at first, I really had trouble believing myself because, although his parents and other family in spirit tried to communicate, he didn't seem to want to hear from them. Then, suddenly, someone called Richard decided to "chip in" and wanted to talk to the sitter. The vicar's response became very enthusiastic and he encouraged the communicator to talk more. The sitting was as usual being recorded and, with the information now being accepted, I continued.

After a while, I was becoming very frustrated because, although this communicator, Richard, was readily answering the questions being asked of him, I did not feel he had clarified his relationship to the sitter. I felt that he was important, but, on asking the identity of the man communicating, I was startled to become aware of a crown being placed before me and to find myself informing the vicar that my communicator was King Richard III – much to the amusement of the vicar who said, "That's right. I'm a member of the Richard III Society."

It appears that he had no relations called Richard, but was hoping that it might be possible to communicate with the King. Since this initial sitting, the vicar has made regular visits every six months over the last four years and each tape has been checked and transcribed. Now I am informed that a book has been published called, "The Secret History – The Truth about Richard and the Princes", in which all the taped sittings will be included.

This is something I have found hard to accept, but since my school history learning was virtually nil, I have to accept the communication in good faith in the hope that it will help towards unravelling some of the unanswered questions of that time so long ago.

Obviously, such surprising incidents teach us that it is perfectly possible to receive communication from whoever chooses to talk to us on this level, no matter how many years they may have been in the spirit world.

Although some sittings are difficult, many are exhilarating, and I have met many interesting people both on earth and in spirit. Through my good friend, David Bexon, who first came to see me for a private sitting, I have been invited many times to give sittings to his friends and associates in London.

David, who has appeared in numerous musicals in the West End and on television, including "The Victoria Wood Show", "The Phantom of the Opera" and "Anything Goes", invited me to see "Anything Goes", whose star was Elaine Paige. David had spoken to her about my work and said that I was seeing the show that evening and I was invited backstage afterwards, which was a privilege. On entering Elaine's dressing room, I felt as if I were stepping back into the 1930s when I saw its marvellous decor. It had a wonderful atmosphere.

The male lead in the show, Howard McGillian, came to join us and, over a drink, Elaine asked me about my gift. We talked about some of the experiences which I have had in my work but interrupted to give Elaine the name of her uncle who was still on the earth-plane, saying that he had not been very well and had terrible trouble with his chest, which Elaine said was true. I followed on with a little more information about him which surprised Elaine in that I could know such things about him.

During the conversation, I turned to Howard, giving him the name of Margaret, his mother, who had passed to spirit from cancer, giving the age of his mother and details of family problems caused by her death. Naturally, Howard was taken aback but was happy to have had the message from his mother in spirit, saying that next time I was in London he would like to see me. However, by the time I returned Howard was in America but he had left me a photograph with a special message on it – "To Bryan. Best wishes; you are amazing. Love, Howard McGillian" which I now keep with Elaine's and others in my room.

Each time now, when I visit London, David has all the sittings arranged and the weekend just sails by, meeting interesting people from many different countries and occupations.

A lovely friend of David's who is a dancer in spirit – Judy – knows of his fellow artistes and always loves to come through with love, laughter and encouragement for them with their careers.

I am very grateful to David for the use of his flat in expanding my work – long may this wonderful opportunity continue!

13th June 1996
HAPPY MEDIUM

Bryan books a chat with Richard III

A newly-published book on Richard III claims to have been written with the king's help aided by Kirkby la Thorpe medium Bryan Gibson.

"Secret History: The Truth about Richard III and the Princes", by the Rev. John Dening was written through four years of sessions with Bryan whom he describes as "one of the finest and most dedicated sensitives of the present era".

From the *Boston and Sleaford Standard*

Chapter Twenty-One

MARILYN

Once their sitting is over, most people who visit my home like to chat and ask questions about my work and experiences. I am often asked whether I talk to anyone famous in the spirit world as my home has two outstanding features – my large collection of cats of all shapes, colours and sizes – and the many photographs of Marilyn Monroe everywhere.

I can still vividly remember the day that Marilyn died while I was still living in London and wondered why her death had made such an impact on me. I do now know why as, since becoming spiritually aware I am able to link up with this very beautiful, but sad, lady being more aware of her at certain times than others, usually when there are going to be articles about her in the press. One instance of this concerned the early days of my spiritual development when, for some strange reason I decided to go out to buy a Sunday paper – which I rarely do – and was driving along when I became aware of Marilyn's voice singing, "I want to be loved by you". As I had no radio on in the car, it just seemed strange but I thought no more about it. After getting home with my newspaper, I did not bother to look at it until much later in the day when I discovered the four centre pages were entirely given over to stories about her, which I later found out she disapproved of, and this was the beginning of my awareness of her and my ability to communicate with her.

These experiences have happened many times since. On one occasion at night, when I was meditating, my attention was kept entirely on her, as if in trance, for at least ten minutes and this was the strongest link with her I had experienced up to that time.

Obviously, I am well aware of the doubts people may feel about making such a statement and realise that we all know a lot about this legendary lady through the films she has made and all that has been written about her, and naturally it is very much open to question. The only real proof of its truth would be to meet someone who knew Marilyn either as Norma Jean or as Marilyn Monroe when she could give personal evidence to which they only could relate.

Although Marilyn is now at peace with herself, she feels very sad that so much is written and spoken about her which is not true and which she is not able to answer in person, but she has now found happiness in the spirit world where she is once more united with all her family, especially her mother about whom a lot has also been said, but they are now at peace together.

Chapter Twenty-Two

MESSAGES ABOUT THE FUTURE

Obviously many people receive messages in sittings at my home or at church services, but that is not the only way. Sometimes people telephone for help, and in the past particularly I have given sittings in this way. I sometimes did this very late in the evening when my time was not so limited, and have not met the people at all on the other end of the line. Even if I could only manage five minutes, I would try to help with guidance for a situation or a pressing problem. Even where the problem is insoluble, a little attention and understanding help a lot.

My telephone rang one night at 11 p.m. The lady ringing had been given my number and needed help. I talked to her about her family and gave her the name of her daughter who had recently passed away from a tumour whilst in her 20s. She gave her mother evidence of her identity, naming family members and mentioning situations to which her mother could relate. She even told her mother that her work would soon change and she would be moving from her mobile home to somewhere new. By the time the conversation ended it was 12.30am as the lady was most reluctant to bring it to an end. Three months later, the lady once again telephoned me but, this time, she was really excited. The message her daughter had given her had been proved correct. She now had a new job and home, even though she had thought it impossible when we had originally spoken, and had made new friends in the fresh environment which she was really enjoying, all as predicted by her daughter.

I try to help, even where the requests are out of the ordinary, such as where someone seeks my assistance in tracing a missing car or, for instance, a lost pet. The requests are all important to the person making them.

Although my spiritual gift is used in many different ways, including the important aspect of healing – my main love is linking up with spirit in bringing the material and spiritual worlds together, enabling families and friends to talk with their loved ones who have passed into the spiritual worlds. However, it is certainly not all solemn; there is also the "fun" side of the work. When information comes through in a sitting which relates to the future, I make sure that sitters realise I pass it on to them, but only if it is shown to me in a very precise and clear way, as I am not a fortune-teller and can only give them the information which is given me.

At the beginning of 1987, a lady called Sylvia came to see me. During the sitting, it transpired that her husband, Jack, and son, Brian, were motorbike riders who had both entered the Manx Grand Prix for that September. At this stage, I proceeded to give off two numbers; one was 47 which I said would be very important, and also the number 9. A few months later, Sylvia came to see me wanting to know more about her son and husband, as it appears that, when they received the entry numbers for the race, her son, Brian, was allocated the number 47 and her husband's number was 109. As the course was difficult and dangerous, Sylvia wanted to know whether they would finish as the bikes were apt to break down on it. My guides became very strong and positive and would only say that Brian would finish in the top ten, the number 7 would bring him luck and, if the weather was sunny and fine, the result could surprise them. When Brian's sister came for a sitting, the same message and numbers were also given to her.

I, too, was delighted and surprised to receive a call at 5.50pm one Thursday from a very excited Sue, relaying a message from her mother in the Isle of Man, to the effect that Brian had actually won the Manx Grand Prix and had broken a lap record. All that I had said had come true.

Another incident where a sitting involved prediction was when a young couple came to see me. Later, we became good friends and regular sitters but it appears that, on the first visit, I told them to be aware of an accident regarding their car. Apparently, I saw their car reversing into something. I said it was not

Relaxing at home with friends after a church service, 1996

dangerous but told them to watch out and gave them a date on which the event would occur. On their next visit, they informed me that everything I had told them was correct. They had been laughing about the fact that the accident I had predicted had not occurred and they thought I had been wrong, but it appears that at 11.45pm on the day in question, John reversed the car out of his drive straight into a van which was not usually parked there. As he said, it really made him feel weird and he commented that next time he would be sure to heed advice from spirit. They both do, finding that spirit guidance is a help in many ways.

Spirit always state that their job is not to live our life for us but they do try to help us on our pathway and it is really satisfying to pass on information which helps in this way and to have confirmation that the prediction has proved true. Where I am concerned, such predictive information comes direct from spirit. This book is written in the hope that it promotes understanding of work such as mine, and of the help which can be given when we lose loved ones. This happens to all of us and we all need comfort, help and guidance in such situations. Everyone of us is capable of being spiritually aware; of working with spirit, for spirit.

Some of us are able to interpret the link with spirit, bringing together the spiritual and material worlds.

We need the insight of our guides and spiritual helpers who are very important parts of our lives. Through them, we learn the ways of spirit and they open up the channels through which our loved ones and friends link up with us. To me, all my guides in spirit are my family who have equipped me with this great gift which cannot be demanded or bought, to use correctly for spirit and never abusing, harming or frightening people in any way. Unfortunately, even this wonderful gift can be used for wrong reasons, such as having power over people. Our lives are ours to make free choices, take responsibility for those choices and learn from the results. When we can do that from a point of Love, in companionship with all our loved ones on earth and in spirit, the results can be wonderful.

If we all walk the pathway using our gifts in such a way, both the present and the future will be very bright indeed.

Chapter Twenty-Three

HELP FROM SPIRIT

Another illustration of the many varied ways used by Spirit concerned a gentleman named Bernard. When they know a particular pathway is the right one for someone here on the earth plane, they can be really persistent in their attempts to help.

Some time ago, Bernard booked to have a sitting with me and when he arrived to see me, we were able to link with his family and friends in the spirit world but he was also hoping for some guidance regarding his current work situation. His family made themselves known to him by name and provided personal messages about his present-day family, also telling me that he wore a uniform connected with nursing but linked, too, with another service and specified that this was the prison service. Bernard agreed that this was correct.

At this stage, a special name was given to Bernard – that of a close family friend named David, who described himself as "a man of the cloth". This pleased Bernard, although he found it very emotional as David had a special place in the hearts of his family. David continued to talk about details of his life and of the memories he had of the special Christmas holidays he always spent with Bernard, his wife (Ruth) and their two daughters and thanked them all for the help and love they had always shown him. David said he felt he could help Bernard with his present-day situation with work. Spirit told Bernard that promotion was on its way for him and Bernard agreed that he had already applied for this but felt that he was doubtful about the outcome due to problems which were in the way of his getting it. Spirit reassured Bernard that, in spite of the problems, he was capable and deserving of the promotion and would get it, so to battle on with the application.

A few months later, I had a 'phone call from a puzzled Bernard who felt that, although he should have got the job, he had been turned down for it, and wondering what he should do now.

At this, Spirit communicated that the result was not final; he should take his situation to a higher authority and not give up. Bernard said that he had already written such a letter and had it there with him but had been unsure whether or not to post it. In view of Spirit's insistence that this was the right path, he said he would go ahead and send the letter.

All this went completely from my mind after that, until the phone rang "out of the blue" one day and it was Bernard. He said, "I had to phone you to thank you and everyone in spirit for all the positive guidance given. After twelve months of fighting, I have now been given the promotion Spirit insisted would be mine. I am so grateful that I followed their suggestions and didn't give in to my own fears."

At that stage, Bernard's friend, David, came through – giving his name and wanting to let Bernard and his family know that both their relatives in the spirit world and he too were very pleased for him. They had been sending out their love and prayers to help him and encourage him to continue, as they knew the result would be positive and that the promotion was indeed Bernard's. Our friends and loved ones continue to care about us after they have left the earth plane; the Spirit World does have a voice if we are listening, and they are truly "just a touch away".

Chapter Twenty-Four

SHOULD I?

Each individual medium has his or her own way of working. As I have already explained, my sitters are always acquainted with my way of doing so before I start bringing through information. I do not believe in pushing my own spiritual awareness on other people when they have not specifically asked for it, and for this reason, do not make a habit of speaking to people about what I may see with them unless there is a very good reason for doing so. I do not receive messages from spirit 24-hours a day and try to ensure that my spiritual strength and energy are channelled in correct ways.

In spite of my belief in not approaching people unasked, there are occasions when spirit are insistent, and one such incident occurred at a local spiritualist church I was attending.

Sitting in front of me, as I sat in the congregation, was a mother with two teenaged children whom I had never before seen. As the service progressed, my thoughts were on these people and I saw a spirit gentleman moving from one to the other during the singing of the hymns and I saw the young man shudder a couple of times whilst the man's hands rested on his shoulders. During the demonstration, the medium came to the lady and said to her, "There is so much love coming to you, but it is too emotional at this time". Leaving it at that, he passed on to the next recipient of a message.

The boy seemed rather perturbed and was whispering to his mother who was doing her best to reassure him.

At this point, my awareness of the service diminished and I was focussed on my spirit family and great emotion and concern for these people became predominant.

As the service ended, I automatically reached out to touch the lady on the shoulder. I apologised to her for approaching her, saying she and I did not know one another, but that I felt I had to ask her whether she had lost a gentleman very recently, aged in his thirties, who had left very suddenly through an accident. They all turned around to look at me as I explained about the man's frustration during the service. As I mentioned the incident with the young man, the spirit man said, "That's my son". They just nodded and the young man hid his face in his hands for a moment, but quickly recovered, saying that he now understood why he had gone so cold a few times. They told me that they had come to the service hoping for some connection with their husband and father, as he had gone to spirit because of a car crash five days before.

The questions started to come thick and fast and the gentleman, now accepted as Jeff, talked about his passing, saying.that he had not suffered as he had left immediately. He gave the name and birth month of his youngest daughter, and talked to his elder daughter about her college work, saying he would watch out for her progress, which she was glad about. Jeff then placed in my hands a guitar, telling me about his love of music – especially the Beatles – which made them laugh – and then told his son he needed to concentrate more when he was playing guitar rather than getting so easily bored, which his son promised to do. Jeff also told his son he would always help him and wanted him to have a silver pocket-watch which had belonged to him and was inscribed. They agreed they knew which of his many watches he meant and Jeff went on to talk about his own father, who was blind but very active and with whom he had worked on making tapes for the blind. He talked about his mother who played the piano for church. It was only at this point that I realised who the family were and that his father had, the previous year, chaired the service for me when I had been acting as medium for a service there. As Jeff said, his parents were very spiritually aware, but it was more difficult for the young people to come to terms with his passing as they needed to understand a little more to bring them peace of mind.

I talked to them a little more of spirit and how their father appeared to me from the spirit world, explaining that when they sent out their thoughts to them, he would be able to hear and hopefully to be able to help them by giving them strength and guidance as he would have done had he remained here on the earth plane.

Although I felt that I had gone against my rule of not passing on messages unasked, I was pleased that spirit had insisted on helping these people in their time of need. It was good to watch them leave the church with their sadness somewhat lifted, smiling now and chatting to each other. It makes everything seem so very worthwhile when things like this happen and I feel very lucky to have been given such a wonderful gift as to be aware of spirit.

Ways are found for spirit to get messages through to those in need whoever is available with the capability of linking up earth with the spirit world, showing that it is just a touch away.

Chapter Twenty-Five

LINKING WITH THE LAW

Spiritual messages often make ripples like water in a pond. It appears that, at one time, I gave a sitter a message about a situation around them which involved the police.

At the time, it seemed just an ordinary message and I gave it no more thought until the person telephoned me a few days later. She was concerned about the fact that she felt she should tell the police about the message but did not want to involve me against my wishes. It did not really mean much to me and I knew very little about the situation which had happened quite a distance away, although I remembered seeing something briefly on television a few weeks previously. Since I do not normally read local papers it all seemed quite vague.

The next day, I received a call from the C.I.D. in that area, explaining that my name had been given and they would like to come to visit me. I agreed to see them the following day and asked them, if possible, to bring along an item connected with the victim to make a stronger connection with the person involved, as this would help with any possible assistance I might be able to give.

As working with the police was new to me, I became a little apprehensive and wondered whether I would get any results at all. Spirit seemed to be confident, even if I was not!

To my relief, the C.I.D. telephoned to postpone the meeting until the day after and, by then, I had become more used to the idea and was no longer nervous about it.

Eventually two C.I.D. officers arrived, bringing with them the appropriate item belonging to the victim. On handling this, I began to give off names and details to them regarding the death, how it happened and what was used, even to describing where it happened in the house and details of objects in it. As I was giving off this information, the two officers just nodded and occasionally looked at each other, so I did not know if I was correct or not. As the sitting progressed, things became much more definite and I began to describe certain items which made them more interested. At the end of the session, the detective constable went to his car and brought back his file, showing me some things which I had correctly described which had never been mentioned outside of the police station, and I obviously had impressed them. They thanked me for my time and I assumed that was the end of the story.

A week later, the C.I.D telephoned again, asking if it was possible for me to go on location with them and if I could possibly do so the following morning. As if by some strange coincidence, it was the only morning that week I had free from sittings and it was obviously kept free for that reason. I agreed and replaced the 'phone and went into the kitchen. All of a sudden, a voice came through with a message which at first I could not quite understand. It was about a bend in the river. As I was not relating to this well, the voice insisted that I wrote it down and I sat promptly with paper in front of me, holding a pen in my hands which started to move, drawing what I can only describe as a plan or a map, adding names to make sure it was correct. I did three which were identical, the last one being most clear. After this, I was left in peace and I returned to my usual routine.

When the C.I.D called to pick me up the next morning, I gave the papers to the detective sergeant, saying, "I do not know what these mean, but it was something I was told to do". On our way to the police station, he seemed to be concentrating on them but said nothing. While I was given a coffee, the detective went to see his senior officer who came down and spoke to me, asking me a few questions, then the detective came back with a rolled map and said to me, "Bryan, it's uncanny, but I will not show you or tell you why till later."

We left the police station for the location. Thankfully, it was a really lovely, sunny day as we were going out into the country. On arriving at the area and getting out of the car, I was able to go to all the landmarks which were very relevant to the case and even to the house concerned where, as I approached, I started to become very agitated and distressed. At this, the detectives asked me if I wished to go on or to leave it, but we continued and, once I had gone past the house, the distress went away. After this, the detectives said, "Now we will show you what was so uncanny about the drawing". On showing me their Ordnance Survey map, I saw I had drawn part of it exactly as shown. It was all within the area concerned and as near to scale as the map, even to the correct bend in the river, the pathway and other notable landmarks. It surprised me that we could be so accurate. I had also learned something – that the person communicating wanted it put in writing, not only as proof to the police that he was communicating through me, but also to show me that I could never have possibly known or guessed at what had been shown me. We then returned to the police station, where I continued to give messages from a photograph given to me. I was given lunch and returned to my home with their thanks.

About an hour later, they telephoned and asked if they could come and see me once more, this time with a tape recorder. They did and once more I linked up with the victim.

This time, he decided to have me experience his death which, at one stage, I had to stop because it made me feel so ill, but the feeling was soon taken away.

He continued to relay messages, mostly the same as he had already said, but confirming certain points which he thought needed more attention.

At one stage, he got very annoyed and I felt that he was so frustrated he wanted to smash things around him, but he eventually calmed down and finished the rest of the sitting.

I could only hope that all this information could help the police in some way to solve the case when everything was complete.

It does show, however, that spirit has the ability to help with current problems when people come to ask for their help. Used properly, everyone can benefit. It is also nice to know that the police will use our services and do not just regard us as "strange people who tell fortunes".

"SPIRIT LED ME"

Medium tells of helping police in murder probe
by Charlotte Beattie

Sleaford Medium Bryan Gibson has told how a dead man's spirit helped trace a man now charged with murder.

Bryan received a telephone call from police asking for his assistance in a murder investigation that shocked a community.

"I wasn't too sure what it was about at first and I felt a little apprehensive. I still agreed as this was a new area of my work," he said. "I must admit I felt nervous and wondered what I'd let myself in for."

On the day of the meeting the police officers produced the dead man's walking stick.

"On handling the stick I began to give the details of the death, the instrument involved, the place in the house and the approximate time of death," said Bryan.

He denies he could have gleaned this information from the media.

"As I'd not read the anything about this incident and only vaguely remember seeing it on TV, I could not have been influenced."

Bryan said at the end of his first sitting with the police officers they returned with a file. They showed the clairvoyant, who sees hundreds of people every year, photos of items he'd described. These had not previously been made public. A week later Bryan received another call from the officers who wanted to meet with him again.

"After I put the phone down a spirit's voice kept repeating a message. It told me to put it in writing, and following its guidance, I drew what appeared to be a map with outlined details, names and places. I did three drawings the last being most positive in detail although otherwise they were all the same," said Bryan.

The following morning Bryan was collected by the police who took him to the scene of the incident.

"We went to the place involved which I'd never seen before in my life. Getting out of the car I was able to point out landmarks. On approaching the victim's house I became very agitated and distressed mentioning certain facts I was receiving about him and his family.

After we had been around the outside of the house and I had walked a little way past the house my distressed state ceased.

The officers then decided to show me their map and it appears the drawings I had done the day before were exact in every detail, even to scale, of the area."

Bryan said the police officers asked him if the spirit wanted the people who committed the crime found, which it affirmed.

"I was then given another item belonging to the victim. The spirit became aggressive and annoyed and started pointing to a person on the photograph giving me certain details.

Later one of the detectives asked me if that was the person involved" said Bryan. "I told him I was certain."

From the *Sleaford Standard*

Chapter Twenty-Six

MISSING

I am glad to say that I get on very well with our local vicar and his family. Fortunately they have an open attitude to my work as a medium and various members of his family have in the past had sittings with me. Therefore, during the years I have known them, we have shared many interesting conversations with regard to the church and spiritualism. We have both learned from each other's knowledge. I do realise, however, that because of my work, their support of me has to be very low key. Many of the local church workers are very anti spiritualism and there have been numerous occasions in the past when they have tried to stop me from doing local charity work in their villages, but have met with little success! Nonetheless, the situation cannot be easy to handle from the point of view of the vicar.

Recently I had a visit from him on behalf of one of his parishioners, asking whether I might be able to help in tracing a lady's husband who had gone missing following a local road accident and who had not been seen since. This followed a call earlier in the day from the man's father asking whether I could help.

Unfortunately, these events took place just as I was preparing to leave for Holland and I suggested that, since I didn't want to start working with them and have to leave the job half done, I would prefer to recommend a very good, local medium named Sue, who I knew would be able to reassure them and hopefully be of some help at such a difficult time for them. Not only is Sue an excellent medium but is also a trained counsellor, so the father contacted her and I left for Holland knowing the matter was in good hands.

On my return, the vicar once again visited me, this time with a sealed envelope containing a photograph and keys, asking whether, as the man still was unfound, I would be willing to help.

I agreed to sit later the same evening to do psychometry on the keys as I had already been aware of the man's grandmother and grandfather in spirit and talked about them to the vicar, adding that at that time, the only message which I was aware of was to the effect, "The water is bothering me. Something is wrong; it's as if a piece of the jigsaw is missing".

I promised that, as soon as I returned in the evening from visiting the people whom I had arranged to see that morning and afternoon, I would work to find out more.

On my return in the evening there was a message on the Answerphone from the vicar saying that the man had been found that afternoon in the water which had been searched the week before, just a distance from where the car crashed. He thanked me for my help and said he would collect the keys and photograph in the morning.

Talking afterwards to Running Foot about the matter, it appeared that the man's grandmother had wanted to communicate to me the fact that her grandson had been missed in the first search and was still in the water and indicating the right place to look. This was the "missing piece of jigsaw" but I was sad that I had not taken time to deal with this, even though Spirit had not pressured me into doing so, knowing that he would shortly be found.

Although, in this case, I was not of much help. it reminded me of the many occasions when relatives of missing people have contacted me, desperate for news of what has happened to their loved ones. One such experience made me very wary on events like this, since it taught me how very difficult it is to remain objective when dealing with people who are very distressed and worried. As mediums, we tread a very fine line on, such occasions – and can make mistakes.

I have a very good friend named Ann, who I have known for more than 20 years. She owned an antique shop and I first met her when buying objects from her shop for my antique stall in Chelsea at that time. The business connection eventually developed into friendship with both Ann and her husband and, although I was still spiritually unaware at that stage, Ann was aware, and I suppose must have been one of my earliest links with Spirit. She, in fact, told me that I would become aware of Spirit myself which I took with a "pinch of salt" and promptly forgot, only to have her remind me years later.

We often shared visits for tea, and the occasional enjoyable day at the coast.

Ann had a son living near her. He was a hairdresser who married a lady – Swedish, I think – with two sons. They emigrated to Australia. Shortly afterwards, much to my surprise, Ann and her husband sold up and moved to Australia to live near her son. By then, I had moved to Lincolnshire and for two years had no contact with Ann. Imagine my surprise on a visit to the area, to be told that Ann had returned home and I was given her address.

We got in touch and, although not a lot was said about the reasons, Ann told me that they had not been able to settle and had decided to return to England. What she was really worried about was the fact that her son had disappeared out of the blue and there was a possibility he had got into difficulty about money and such-like. Obviously, all sorts of possibilities were considered, even to the extent of wondering whether he had taken his own life, but over the years no body turned up and no word was received from him. However, Ann never gave up trying to trace him, advertising in the press and even putting up posters.

After some time, I think Ann came to feel that he was no longer with us and, whenever I visited, would give me things of his to hold and ask me to see if I could get any communication about him.

Mostly, I just felt he was still alive – possibly in New Zealand – but didn't want to be found and, although she appeared accepting of this, deep down was unsure I had got it right. Eventually, of course, she desperately wanted a definite answer and there came a time when she gave me his wallet to hold. On that occasion I felt that his father was communicating with me (Ann's first husband who had been in spirit for some time) and, feeling under extreme pressure to come up with something definite I told her that I felt her son was in spirit too, and she said she also felt this to be true.

A considerable time later, on a visit to Ann's house, I was doing sittings at her home and she smiled and told me, "You didn't get everything right with me last time!" Not thinking it was anything important, I smiled and got on with tea. It was later that I learned from John, who was with me, that, whilst I was out of the room, she had told him that her son had in fact been seen at last, but didn't want any contact with his family, so that was the end of the search.

Naturally, she didn't want to upset me, but I felt absolutely awful at having got such an important message wrong, and I had to sort out with Running Foot how this could have happened, realising it would have been better had I stayed with my original impression rather than feeling I had got it wrong and coming to a totally wrong conclusion.

Running Foot explained to me how I had picked and identified with the strength of Ann's feelings that he was in spirit for one thing, but had also mistaken the son's strong sense of wanting to maintain the separation and not being found as of being already out of reach in spirit, wrongly interpreting the feelings as, not just of deliberate separation, but of being separated by physical death.

Obviously I was at fault for making such a statement without really doubt-checking with my spirit helpers and this situation unsettled me for quite a while and I still feel guilty about it and still have to make a point of sitting down and discussing it with Ann, so shall have to see to that as a matter of urgent importance.

It is difficult to help people in such distress anyway, but when the people involved are known to you in any way, it is even more difficult particularly if they are close friends. Obviously the lesson must have made a considerable impact on me, as now, in such cases I always try to point people in the direction of another medium rather than make the same mistake again.

We never stop learning!

Chapter Twenty-Seven

PROBLEMS YET TO BE SOLVED

Just because I am a working medium or a spiritually aware person, does not mean that others should assume I have all the answers. I do not. It would be very nice to say, "Yes. I have the answers to all questions placed before me and I understand all the spiritual experiences I have undergone", but it would not be true.

There are many questions I have still unanswered and there are things which I have experienced which I still do not understand myself and, like other people, shall have to wait until either the time is right, or the necessary person contacts me either on the physical level or from spirit to help me to understand. Nothing is as instant as we often want it to be, and many times we need a great deal of patience before the right moment arrives and we have the ability to understand what puzzles us.

This has often applied to me, but there are two outstanding experiences which, for me, still await clarification. One happened to me recently, the other some years ago. The earlier one had passed to the back of my mind really until the recent event, which reminded me of it.

In June 1996 I made a visit to the Spiritualist Association of Great Britain in Belgrave Square in London. I was booked to work there from the Tuesday until the Thursday night, giving sittings and demonstrations. Visiting mediums are provided with rooms which are now situated at the top of the building, so we both work and sleep in the same building. It had been a pleasant, but uneventful week, with plenty of work and pleasant occasions together with other mediums catching up with old times and stories.

My work finished on Thursday, I was to stay overnight and return home on the Friday, but the next morning proved memorable.

The only other visiting medium staying overnight was Kathleen Knaggs, so she and I were alone in the building. I got up at about 8 am and, having plenty of time to spare before catching my coach home, planned to pay a visit to my publisher and browse around Oxford Street before going home.

I knew that Kathleen planned to go out early to have her hair done at the hairdresser's and was not surprised to find myself the only person in the building.

At around 8.45 am, following a shower and some tea and toast, I left for the bus-stop without a jacket, but as it started to rain I decided to go back for one.

To enter the SAGB, you have to descend steps to the basement door and, in order to open it, press in a series of numbers which allow you entrance. I used the lift and stairs to the mediums' rooms, collected my jacket and returned downstairs. The building is very peaceful and so quiet that I should certainly have heard any noise or sound around.

As I approached the door to go out and opened it, I came face to face with a very well-dressed man aged around 40, wearing a very smart green, double-breasted suit, and my first thought was, "I really like the suit!" His shirt was white with a plain tie and he looked very much the typical office person. Although, initially, we both appeared startled, I remember that, as I opened the door, his hand was raised as if he was just about to place his key in the lock, and it was as if we both opened the door at the same time. I remember saying, "Good morning" and he responded with a smile and a nod and, as I stood aside for him to pass by before closing the door, turned and watched him walk down the corridor and disappear, My initial thought was, "I didn't know the office staff started so early". Usually, they started arriving just before 10 am and dressed casually, so the man stood out being both early and unusually immaculately dressed.

I forgot the incident as I caught the bus to Holborn and discovered that my publisher was not in that day, so left a message for him and took a long, steady stroll along Oxford Street prior to catching a bus back to the SAGB. By now, Kathleen was back from the hairdresser's and we sat and had a chat together over a cup of tea. When I mentioned the earlier incident to her, Kathleen said, "Ask Bob and Julie in the kitchen if they know who he is", and I did so. My description of the man produced only totally blank looks and they assured me that, apart from Glen on the desk, the rest of the office staff were women. I went to look at the photographs in the corridor of the committee and mediums serving the SAGB, but once again found no similarity whatever.

The people on the desk, of course, knew everyone using the building, and I spoke to them, about it, describing what had happened. Chris looked at me and asked, "Did you hear the door buzz before you opened it?" which I had not. In response to my describing the visitor as having his hand raised to put the key in the lock, the response was, "There hasn't been a lock used in the door for years; it's always been the press-coded locking system and no-one could get in that way".

The story was getting weirder and weirder; no-one could even suggest who the visitor could have been. So far, the only explanation I can come up with is that I was lucky enough to be at the right place at the right time to meet a very lovely spirit being entering the SAGB. Perhaps in the past he had worked there and still felt part of it, but he certainly was not old and he was very smartly dressed. I am only sorry I took no greater notice of him and didn't have a conversation with him at the time. Perhaps on my next visit to the SAGB I may have the honour of seeing him again or at least find out something about him. I hope he appeared to me for a reason and maybe I shall discover it later.

The story did have a sequel about a week later. About 6 weeks previously I had ordered a suit having just picked out the colour from a sample, and when I collected the new suit and opened it, found a double-breasted, green suit exactly like I had seen the man at the SAGB wearing. If there are indeed no such things as coincidences, was this a sign that I am to await further developments?

The whole sequence of events reminded me forcibly of the previous experience I mentioned which had happened to me about seven years before. For some reason, I did not mention it to anyone then but what happened was that I simply went to buy myself a newspaper one Sunday morning. It was around 9 am – I think it was November – and I remember that, as I drove towards the main street, it was very foggy and I saw what appeared to have been an accident which I presumed had occurred during the night. An old beige Austin car was embedded in the side window of the jeweller's shop. The window appeared to have fallen and chopped the car in half and all that was visible was the back seat and boot of it which was covered with a large tarpaulin. I remember thinking, "That looks nasty; I wonder if anyone was killed". As I drove alongside, my attention was caught by a man standing on the opposite side of the road by a men's clothes shop. He stood in the doorway wearing a mac and a trilby hat and was carrying a large camera of a sort not seen nowadays.

He was shrouded by the mist, and thinking no more of it, I drove home. Later in the afternoon, I again went into Sleaford and passed the scene of the accident. When I got there, there was no car, no damaged shop window and no doorway opposite, only a shop window. I thought, "They have cleared that all up quickly; it will be in the paper on Thursday and I shall find out more about it". At the time I was living alone and knew very few people in the town, so had no-one to discuss it with when the Thursday paper arrived without any mention of the accident, and the matter faded from my mind. I definitely saw the whole thing in detail and I don't know why I have not talked about it before, but it was probably to protect myself from other people thinking me "mad", but of course I now realise that there must be a record of such an accident happening, so I have promised myself I shall try to find out what did happen. Someone must know – and mediums are allowed to see things which aren't physically there! By the make and shape of the car, it would have to be the 50s era, so at least there is somewhere to start with finding out details.

These two widely-spaced experiences are personally important to me although I haven't talked much about them before. Perhaps the time was not right to do so then, but now I am perhaps a little wiser and spiritually more mature, maybe I can discover the facts and enable others to know that "seeing things" is not necessarily dreaming, nor imagination, but part of that wonderful, greater reality of which we all are a part.

Chapter Twenty-Eight

WHERE TO NOW?

We have looked at different kinds of communication between the spirit world and this, but what does this teach us?

My wonderful friend, "Running Foot" tells me that life in the spirit world is full of love, understanding, guidance and progress, with the chance to go and progress to a higher and better insight of life and development, and to devote time and energy to helping others.

We all reach out for help to someone who has more knowledge and understanding than we do. I myself am guided by Running Foot, but we also both have a higher guide who comes to help us and guide us when we need that extra strength and knowledge. The name of our leader is "Mankin" who, when on earth, was a buddhist monk, and who has been in the world of spirit for many generations.

He is not only a very wise and knowledgeable person, he is also very gentle and understanding and many times comes to help us when we cannot find a solution or answer to a question. He watches over us and is always there when I am giving a talk during a church service. On occasions when I have closed my eyes and allowed him to come through to talk to the people in his own voice, he passes on his own learnings from within the spirit world. Each time we learn a little more from him and he gives us reasons to think about life and to progress.

In spirit, there are no differences based on race, religion or status such as cause most of the problems of earth. In the world of spirit, love, harmony and truth prevail and it is very sad that life on earth is so unlike that.

As I understand from spirit, the life we live on earth is very important for our spiritual progress. On earth, we have to experience the whole scope of human experience – love, hate, sadness, jealousy, pain, fear, misunderstanding and adventure. When we have experienced all of these, then only are we a complete person and at peace with ourselves. If, while on earth, we have not completed all of these experiences, I am told by spirit, we are given another chance to return to earth to complete our life-cycle. As an example of what I mean, it is like when a person is brought into the world and stays only for a very short time, maybe weeks or months and may suffer even during such a short stay. It probably fulfils the one experience which was left unfulfilled before and was necessary for completion of the soul's experience and understanding, enabling the person now to progress in spirit.

We come to terms with ourself. I know that I have now found that peace of mind. In the experiences of my life, each and every one has had a purpose and, although I may not have understood what was happening at the time, I am slow to make the same mistakes again.

Now my wonderful gift has been proved to exist for a definite reason, not only for my own understanding but also to enable me to relate to each person, as walking through the pain and ecstasy of life's pathway enables us to understand other people's needs.

I know I shall look forward to my transition into the world of spirit, not with fear and uncertainty, but looking forward to the love reaching out to me and bringing me into the continuation of a future to come. I know I shall never lose contact with my loved ones left behind, and shall look forward to eventually joining with them when they also return to the world of spirit.

Man has always had a dream, a dream of a beautiful world where the beauty and love and truth of the spirit worlds is brought into being here on earth. We are a long way from that dream today, but those in spirit are still working to make that beautiful dream a reality on this earth plane and still watch for those of us who will work with them to make it so.

The choice is ours, for the dream is already a reality in the spirit worlds and it can be here if we will it so; together we can create it, for truly they are all only a touch away.

Chapter Twenty-Nine

GERMANY

Every year presents us with a new beginning. As a medium, I always hope for improvement in my work from the previous year. There is always the chance of progressing along the spiritual pathway and both learning more about people in general and about spiritual communication in particular, so when opportunities present themselves for this, it is always exciting.

1996 was, for me, a year of pleasant progress. Because I am stubborn, I have always said that I'm happy doing the work I am doing and have no wish to change either my way of working or my routine – but 1996 changed all that.

Through demonstrating at the S.A.G.B in Belgrave Square in London in June 1966, I met a special lady who gave me the chance of taking my mediumship a step further. Lilo Meyer is an interpreter who visited the S.A.G.B. from Germany, sitting in on consultations to interpret messages for people from Switzerland and Germany.

Following the third sitting, Lilo approached me to ask whether I would be willing to visit Frieburg in Germany to work in her home. I was happy to agree, explaining that I had no experience of doing workshops, but would gladly do private sittings or demonstrations. Lilo promised to telephone me at a later date to organise the visit and, before long, everything was arranged for me to work in Frieburg during October 1966. However, Lilo still wanted me to do a workshop as well and I, therefore, somewhat half-heartedly, said I would do so. I was excited about the visit, but anxious about the workshop, but put the material for this together with the encouragement of John, Maureen and Sue who offered to help with it, saying that it was easy and simple for people to do! It was decided that the first half should focus on introducing people to their guides and the second on auragraphs, so eventually, with the help of my friends, notes and crayons, everything was prepared and ready for Germany.

I need not have worried! My new journey began and I was met at Basle Airport by Lilo and Karl Heinz. The first few days were spent giving private sittings and, with Lilo's great assistance, everything went very well. Although very few people spoke English, there were no hiccups due to Lilo's wonderful interpreting and everything was well accepted.

A day out with Lilo Meyer and Andrea during my hectic working trip to Freiburg, Germany, 1997

Wednesday was to be "Demonstration Night" and was arranged to take place in rooms belonging to Benjt Jacoby, a friend of Lilo's, which were part of an alternative therapy clinic. The room for the demonstration itself proved to be lovely – very spiritual – and filled to capacity with around sixty people. As the evening got underway, there was a lot of laughter and amusement, particularly when animals came through from spirit, and at times I got carried away with my communication and was so enthusiastic that Lilo had to keep nudging me and reminding me that she could not remember it all if I didn't stop for a few sentences, which made everyone laugh even more.

It was a great night and resulted in requests for private sittings which filled up my last free day available before returning home.

The workshop was scheduled for the Saturday and I was still nervous about it. My doubts about my capability of making a success of it increased as I realised the numbers due to be attending! Again, I need not have worried. Everyone was very receptive and eager to learn and I was surprised at the extent of their desire to develop and at how well they linked with their guides and meditated. In fact, we overran the allotted time and managed to be late for lunch!

The afternoon session surprised me even more. Their progress and the truly wonderful auragraphs they produced are unforgettable. I felt that I had myself taken another step on my own spiritual pathway and everyone went home happy, sad only because they had to wait for the next workshop to take place.

So, my visit to Germany was a great "first" for me. I truly value the friendship and help of Lilo, Karl Heinz and Emmy, as well as her grand-daughter Andrea, with whom I spent a special day out in the Black Forest before returning home and I look forward to maintaining contact with these special new friends. Maybe, on my return to their country, I may have learned a little more German.

Having thought that was the end of my connection with Germany for the moment, imagine my astonishment when, two weeks later, I found myself back at the S.A.G.B working with numerous German people, this time with a different interpreter helping me to communicate between spirit and visitors from the area around Dusseldorf. This time it seemed easier and I was able to show off my new-found confidence, even understanding a few German words myself, and positively understanding what was said more quickly than previously.

Now I am eager to be more adventurous. I feel I shall not hesitate if any more foreign opportunities come my way, so here's to 1997!

We all have to learn how to communicate well, whether it is with people on the earth-plane or those on other levels of consciousness, like our friends and loved ones in spirit. It is indeed "good to talk". As we move into the next century, no doubt new and exciting methods of communicating with each other will emerge. Let us look forward to that and resolve to make sure we use all these means to express love and light, truth, beauty and goodness in all our communicating. When we do that, we all shall be mediums operating "Spirit's telephone exchange" and life will become the richer and the sweeter for that.

Chapter Thirty

"CENTURY RADIO"

In my chapter about my visit to Germany, I said how the experience made me eager to become more adventurous and to spread the news of my spirit world farther afield.

Little did I know how suddenly that would be put into action; once again my spirit work would be challenged and put to the test.

Whilst I was working in Germany, John, my manager, received a call from John Symons – a presenter and director of a commercial radio station called "Century Radio" in Gateshead.

John Symons wanted to know, whether I would be interested in having a regular, live phone-in spot on the radio. Apparently, over three and a half years before, when John Symons was a presenter with Nottingham Radio, he interviewed me and I gave him evidential proof of his Grandfather in spirit which impressed him so much that he kept my name and telephone number in his diary. When the opportunity arose, he phoned to contact me. John phoned me in Germany with the news, suggesting that I think about it until my return home, when he would deal with the matter,

My immediate response was one of excitement, but once I began to think about it, doubts began creeping into my mind and I decided to postpone a decision until I had discussed it with people who know both me and my work.

When I got back from Germany, John explained more about the situation. Apparently, the radio station had been presenting mediums live at various times, but had been unhappy with the recent programmes and John Symons had said that they urgently needed what he saw me as being . . . a "genuine medium".

Both John Brett and another friend I discussed it with, were convinced that I was capable of doing the show, pointing out the benefits of my work becoming known in a part of the country I had not yet visited, but I was still unsure in spite of how exciting the possibility was, and how easy everyone made it sound!

Eventually I talked with John Symons and, after much persuasion, agreed to do it, fixing a starting date in November to coincide with a planned visit to Scarborough one Sunday. He then asked me for an update of details of my work and a copy of my book to be sent to the particular presenter who would be doing the show. Unfortunately, when this presenter telephoned me one evening, I did not find his attitude very spiritual, feeling all the time that he was trying to get me to give him some sort of sitting over the telephone – which would have been the worst thing I could have done, in fact. I knew by then that the programme was designed to last for two hours, with the medium giving messages to people for the duration of the phone-in, with the presenter overseeing everything and linking it all together, and, as I came off the telephone, I had the strongest conviction that l could not work with this man.

Everyone felt, I think, that I was being silly and negative since they were all totally convinced that I could do it, but, as the days passed my fears and anxieties became stronger, rather than less, and I finally announced that I could not do it.

John telephoned the radio station once more, explaining to John Symons about my decision and the reason for it. John Symons replied, "Tell Bryan that I will present the first show with him if that will help, because we know each other and I know Bryan is the right person for our show."

In spite of all the pressure to do it, my gut feeling still remained unaltered. I knew I was throwing away a marvellous chance of expanding my work and making my name known, but felt it was the right decision not to do it unless I was confident of presenting myself properly, as I had no desire to make a complete mess of everything.

From the moment I said, "No", I felt better. I was again at peace with my work and felt Spirit had guided me correctly. December passed peacefully in spite of further calls from John Symons. However, he telephoned yet again in January 1997, stating that he still wanted me for the show and that they now-had a new presenter for the show named Roger Kennedy, and asking that I give them one more chance.

To my own great surprise, I agreed, and a date was fixed for Monday, February 17th 1997. This time, I decided not to talk to the presenter beforehand, but to just go ahead and do the show. During the period leading up to the radio show, I felt really relaxed, not worried or nervous as I had felt before. Since I was to travel up by train, it meant a really early start, getting up at 6.30 am and leaving Grantham at 8.09 am. John decided to make the journey with me to give me moral support (and, I think, to make sure I didn't back out!). Thank Goodness he did! The morning's travel was disasterous; the train was delayed at Doncaster and, as the time ticked by, we could see no way of ever arriving in time for the show. John managed to phone the station from the train and they said, "O.K., get here when you can, even if the show has started".

At last the train arrived at Newcastle station. The time was 11.53 am and we still did not know how far the radio station was from the railway station. We jumped into a taxi to find that the station was nearby and arrived with just minutes to spare, as Roger Kennedy was about to go on air. There was no time for introductions, just "Hello. How are you?" and that was that. Next minute, before I realized it, I was in the studio, sitting with headphones on to Roger's voice introducing me.

I still was not really aware of the show's format or what I was required to do but, before I could start worrying about that, a lady's voice came over the headphones saying, "Hello, Bryan. Have you a message for me?" and lo and behold, it worked! The messages from spirit came through loud and clear and were accepted positively. The communicator in spirit was recognised and the information was relevant to the lady. The next caller was put through and this continued, one after the other for two hours, interrupted only for the occasional advertisement and by the news on the hour, apart from Roger's conversation with each caller confirming that what I had said was correct and that they understood the loving messages from communicators in spirit.

By the end of the show, it appeared that I had given twenty-two messages with no rejections of what I had said, everybody appearing to understand the information from spirit. I felt great. It was like being in another world . . . another exciting phase in my spirit work had begun.

Each caller was allowed only, to give their first name and say, "Have you got a message for me?" I did not realise how easy it was to link this way and, as a medium, it was the best confidence booster imaginable. There was no possibility of reading body language, eye contact or being fed information. It was elating . . . pure magic!

John Symons was waiting outside to congratulate me, along with John and Noddy from the switchboard. It appears that the switchboard was jammed and an estimated 25,000 callers had tried to get through. Even after the show, people were still phoning the station.

Roger Kennedy was the perfect person to work with. He was easy to talk to and, what pleased me most was that he just joined in with the messages, checking if I was correct and laughing with the humourous moments which arose. It was two hours of joy which I shall never forget. Once again, Spirit had given me the love and strength to do their work. Without hesitation, John Symons and Roger Kennedy asked me for a date when I could return and it was agreed that I would do it in March, followed by fortnightly programmes from April onwards. This was the period during which the station survey figures were compiled and, since our show was producing an estimated 50,000 calls including people telephoning from Sunday on, it was seen as a potential boost for them. People were calling before I got there each Monday and the contacts made have become the basis of real friendship. One caller from the first programme who received a message on air – Steve Nee – wrote to the station, making his home at our disposal if we wished to stay in Newcastle or to give sittings there . . . an offer of which we gratefully took advantage.

It has all provided the opportunity to make regular visits to Newcastle and the North-East, meeting with the warm and friendly, lovely Geordie people. Staying with Steve has meant that, although my breakfast is normally tea and toast, I have to eat a "proper Geordie breakfast"; they certainly make sure you are fed well!

Apart from Steve and his sister Maureen, there are many people who have been very supportive and it is difficult to mention them all. Nonetheless, I do feel I must mention special friends, Christine, Ann, Hilda, Lynn and Lorraine who have made a point of sitting together with their tea and "cigs" listening to the show, as well as particularly mentioning Hilda's husband, Cecil, who from morning to night – listens to Century Radio and, it appears, is a great fan of the midday phone-in. Our thanks to them all for their love and support.

The opportunity this invitation provided has given me the challenge needed to expand my work for Spirit. It is something which I shall remember always.

Chapter Thirty-One

THE SITTING

Through recent experiences which I have encountered during sittings at home and on my last visit to the S.A.G.B. (Spiritualist Association of Great Britain), I feel it would be good to explain about how sittings work and how the sitter can help.

Obviously, for all of us, there is a first time of meeting a spiritualist medium; on such occasions we are unsure what to expect and it always helps to know what is going on.

Some mediums, when giving the sitting, explain how they work, what they require from the sitter, and how the communication from their contact in spirit works. They explain that it is a three-way link between the medium, the sitter and the spirit communicator.

It is good for the sitter to respond to the messages given by the medium with a simple "yes" or "no" without feeding the medium with extra information, as otherwise it is not possible for the spirit communicator to prove who is communicating. For instance, a sitter saying, "Yes; that's my Dad and he died from cancer" prevents the medium giving that fact direct from spirit and thereby confirming to the sitter that it really is his Dad providing the information.

Also, in situations where a medium asks a sitter who they wish to hear from, although the medium may then get a link with spirit, if I were the sitter in question I should certainly think, "Yes, what the medium is saying is right, but I'm not sure whether they have really come through".

What we have to remember to tell our sitters is, linking with spirit is an experiment where nothing is guaranteed and it is not possible for any medium to give specific evidence on request of the sitter. A medium's work is to try to provide people on the earth plane with evidence of survival of loved ones in spirit, and not to predict the future. People in spirit have the same freedom as we do on the earth plane as to whether to choose to communicate with us. No sitter can demand who they wish to talk to and unless such a person wishes to use the channels opened up by the medium to come through and talk, they will not do so. However, before arriving for the sitting, a sitter can send out love and thoughts to those in spirit, asking them to come and talk to them and there is no reason why they should not do that.

My sitters find that I explain how I work and what they may expect. As I only know the first name of the sitter, we introduce ourselves to each other and set up a tape if they have brought one with them to record the sitting. I then explain the way in which I work, talking about the fact that memories and events in their past and present-day life may be mentioned and telling them not to be surprised that the spirit communicator has so much knowledge of their life. Although the family is paramount (and, where people live together, it is accepted as a marriage), I also point out that the names given may not always be family members, but also the names of people they worked with or of friends and others who have meant something to them, the spirit communicator showing by such means that he or she is still around and up to date with what is going on in the sitter's life. Months are often given which relate to family birthdays or anniversaries – sometimes a month is mentioned when a person passed into spirit – or occasionally a future date when something is planned to take place in a sitter's life.

I explain to the sitter that, if they have someone in spirit who wishes to come through and talk with them, with me they always try to give me how they left for spirit, describing a health condition or "accident", followed by details of whether they are family members and who they are or specifying that they are a workmate or other similar information in order to identify themselves.

Once they have been accepted, communicators may perhaps encourage sitters to push forward in a new direction if this is appropriate, or even to nicely tell them off as they would have done had they still been here on the earth plane. I follow on this explanation by saying that all I require of the sitter is a simple "yes" or "no" in response, or confirmation that they understand what is being said. I ask that no information be fed to me, saying that if I make mistakes in the sitting, I shall be corrected by spirit. This enables the sitter to relax and the communication is enabled to flow freely between the three links.

This is the way in which I like to work, and I find that it enables sitters to be relaxed and positive. It also means that no time gets wasted in the sitting and that everyone knows what to expect and can fully cooperate with what is going on.

On occasion, barriers can be put up by a sitter who has someone in spirit with whom they do not wish to talk. Sometimes the problem is that they do not want certain things to be mentioned. Spirit mostly respect this and, knowing what the sitter wants, will try to answer their doubts and fears at the same time as reassuring them that they are happy and at peace in the spirit world.

I should now like to give a few examples of what can go wrong in a sitting and how barriers can be erected.

Recently, whilst I was working at the SAGB, a gentleman named Tony was booked for a sitting with me. After explaining the way I worked to him, the taped sitting began. He could accept the first communication with a workmate who had recently left for spirit due to a heart attack. This link established, the message continued about work and the spirit communicator said that Tony had decisions to make about shift changes which he agreed was correct. His mate's advice was that it was time for a change, saying that it wouldn't be a bad idea for Tony to make the move. However, Tony said, "I'm sorry. I cannot accept that because we both worked on the same shift and he was very much against changing from nights to days." The spirit communicator explained to me that that was when he was on the earth plane but that, now he was in spirit, he could see both sides and felt his advice was right. Tony said, "O.K" and the next message from the communicator involved a yellow fork-lift truck and what appeared to be a factory or large warehouse. On asking the sitter whether this made any sense to him, he quickly said "No" but the message and picture was still there. On explaining to Tony it was still being given to me, I asked whether he was sure it didn't relate, and was once more answered by a strong, "No!", followed on by, "Unless I'm going to be using one, but we haven't any here . . ." I could feel the tension coming in as my spirit cormnunicator was not changing the message and I couldn't let it go. I said, "Well, Tony, it has to mean something because I'm still being given the same information." After a little while, Tony finally said, "Well, opposite where we work, there is a warehouse with a yellow fork-lift truck but I don't see it as I'm on night shift." I explained that this was his mate's way of confirming his identity by describing where they worked and giving me an image of the working surroundings.

I could see that there was no way that Tony was going to accept this information and explained to him that I did not think it was worthwhile continuing with the sitting as doubts had crept in. I felt that Tony was going to accept only things he wanted to hear and it was best he was taken back to the desk and either have his money returned or have a sitting with another medium who might be better able to communicate for him.

During the same period of time, I had a lady named Barbara who was booked for a one-hour sitting. She was a very nice lady and, once again, I explained my work and began communicating with spirit. The first communicator was her father and she grudgingly said "yes", although I could see from her face that she was not happy. Then came her mother and her husband, but her father was very dominant and insisted on talking first. I felt he wanted to apologise to his daughter but, after a few messages, Barbara was becoming very annoyed. She explained that she "didn't want her Dad; she didn't like him and she didn't want to talk with him". I asked him to let someone else through but each time he kept interrupting and the barriers with Barbara were being put up, so I explained to her that I had to allow her father to talk as otherwise he would not let anyone else through, but she insisted that she didn't want him. As I couldn't see me giving Barbara a sitting for an hour with anything she wanted, I said, "Sorry, but I cannot work with this sitting" and Barbara also went back to the desk and arranged to see another medium in the hope of getting more from her Mum and her husband. I talked afterwards to the second medium she saw and apparently they had the same trouble. The sitting was completed, but Barbara's father still came through.

By showing these experiences, it will be obvious that we do not always get the messages we wish. People in spirit don't change; they can still be as strong and bossy as when on the earth plane and, if they still want to annoy us, they can. However, their need to communicate with us often relates to their overwhelming desire to be forgiven for things said whilst on the earthplane with us. Where we are still angry with them, it is as important for us as it is for them to accept their love and apologies. Forgiveness enables peace to be made and we can move forward free. Bad feeling ties us as strongly to another person as does love and if we want to be free of such connections, then it is a very good idea to settle for forgiveness; otherwise, we still have to suffer the consequences until we do.

These things need to be remembered when you go for a sitting. Keep an open mind. Make sure that you look farther afield than just family as names mentioned can belong to anyone connected to you or yours, and even those communicating from spirit may not be directly involved with you. I have known a number of occasions when sittings were used to pass on a message second-hand to someone known to the sitter in the hope of getting a message to a loved one when needed.

Animals and special events in your life will also be likely to get a mention and, as I always say, spirit people love to gossip with us. Having a sitting is just like sitting in a room, having a cup of tea and a chat, and going over old times as well as talking about things still to come.

As they say, "Memories are made of this" . . .

Chapter Thirty-Two

FOR POPPY

Saturday, March 7th 1998 is a day which I shall never forget. It was a day on which I had to make a decision such as I had not dreamed of ever making.

Our lovely cat, Poppy, had been ill on and off for over two years. All possible help and love had been given her, but she still seemed to be unwell even though the vet could not find anything seriously wrong. Since Christmas '97 she had seemed worse, but kept appearing to be back to her normal self after each bout of illness lasting a few days at a time.

At the end of February '98, whilst I was away working at the S.A.G.B., John kept me in touch with how she was. Poppy seemed to be getting worse and was eating very little, so we arranged for her to be seen by the vet on Saturday, 7th March when I returned home. On our arrival at the vet's, she was examined by the owner of the practice who quickly diagnosed her condition and told us that it had now affected her nervous system. She was therefore unable to control all her

Our very special cat, Poppy

natural functions and it was obviously causing her distress. I therefore was faced with having to make the awful decision about whether to prolong her life and suffering, or to take the responsibility for bringing it to an end. She was much loved and we did not feel it was fair to cause her any more suffering, so – very emotionally, and through many tears – I took the decision to end her life. I could not stay with her for the fatal injection; it was left to John to do so, and he was a very great support. Poppy was brought home and buried with love in the garden, where she now has a lovely azalea bush growing for her. We have also just planted poppy seeds there, so her part of the garden will always be colourful.

It is still very hard to accept Poppy's passing. She was just 13 years old and was a great favourite with all the sitters. Every day I am aware of her presence and still talk with her. Occasionally, when out shopping, I have still got her food before realising she no longer needs it, and it has had to be given to the hedgehogs who come calling. They no doubt appreciate it!

I felt that I should like this tribute to Poppy to be included in the book as she has been written about in previous books and people still ask after her.

I thought it was a lovely touch that Colin Cummings, the vet, and his staff sent a card expressing their sadness and thoughts for us, a few days after her passing, I doubt whether there are many veterinary surgeries who include this very spiritual touch as part of their service, and it helped a great deal. We also received cards from some of our friends when she passed.

Poppy will never be forgotten . . . and, one day, we shall be reunited.

Tribute to Poppy

Sedately, through the door she walked,
With tail held high and a haughty look,
Then sat defiantly by her tray
And a look to match that seemed to say,
"Well . . . aren't you feeding me then today?"

Another day and another pose,
Through the kitchen and lounge
On paw-tip toes.
Slow and deliberate,
Sideways on . . .
Fooling an unseen audience.

To a wild leap with claws outstretched,
The cushion submitted to feline attack.
Satisfied, she licked her paw,
Then kicked her victim to the floor.

In quieter mode, she lay on the mat,
With a roll to the left and right
Then hooked her weary leg onto mine.
"Pick me up" her eyes would implore.

Then into the crook of my arm she slid
And curled in a perfect ball.
To a purr of contentment whispered here
While the 'phone purred out in the hall.

Then shuddered out of my senses
By the urgency of her flight,
I saw Poppy, the fearless wonder cat
As proud hunter of the night.

Sadly, she's no longer with us
And I miss the antics she played.
"A PROPER LITTLE MADAM"
I'll remember all my days.

(Bless you, Poppy!)

(For Bryan, by Paul Underwood)

POEMS

It is a great pleasure for me to meet people both on the earth plane and from spirit. I find it rewarding when people not only contact me by letter but also send me poems which they have written, often when they have had a sitting with me and feel the urge to put pen to paper. These poems are very personal to the people involved and I feel honoured to have helped in some small way towards linking these people with their loved ones in spirit.

There are also other mediums, as well as people who themselves are developing spiritually, who do inspirational writing and feel their words may help others, seeing myself as a bridge for their words to be heard by my readers. I hope their words will not only reinforce the sense of their connectedness to their own loved ones in spirit but also reach out to those seeking guidance and help on their pathway, whether material or spiritual.

I hope therefore that you all will enjoy this collection of poems and I am very grateful for being allowed to share them with you.

* * *

The following poem was presented to me already framed when the lady came to see me for a private sitting, and now hangs in my room for everyone to see.

The Medium

I met this person named Bryan Gibson
Who is a very gifted man
He brings a lot of comfort
To folk whenever he can.

Now I was a bit of a sceptic
Like many people seem to be.
My daughter, who is a firm believer
Said, "Mum, why don't you come and see?"

I agreed to go along with her
And was very, very impressed.
I had seen a few other mediums
But Bryan was far the best.

It isn't morbid, or even sad
Like people seem to think.
The spirits come through happily
With messages that tickle you pink.

It's not just the messages that he gets
It's the way he knows who they're for.
He totally amazes me
I want to hear more and more.

He really is most convincing
With names and knowledge of you;
The personal things – and memories
That only you know are true.

The spirit world is a happy one
Where animals also have a place
You can see everyone enjoys themselves
By the look on Bryan's face.

He tries to answer them one by one
Which can't be an easy task.
Then he passes on their messages
Of things in the present and past.

Seasons of Life

Four seasons God has granted
To help mankind to grow.
The first one he called SPRING
So we could set and sow.

The second sent was SUMMER
To give us warmth and light.
He then blew radiant sunshine
To make days long and bright.

The third he gave was AUTUMN
To show we're fully grown,
But soon we will be tested
With rain and wind that's blown.

But WINTER is the hardest,
When dark clouds loom above,
For then mankind will truly feel
The great power of his love.

Four seasons sent to give us
The chance of life anew;
His love and guidance He will give.
The rest is up to you . . .

MONICA

My Son

A darling baby boy so new,
He stole my heart with eyes of blue.
And then a toddler, cute and dear,
He kept my heart, year after year.

All through his school years,
A bright boy,
He filled my heart with pride and joy.
Through adolescent teenage years,
We'd share his doubts, and share his fears.

Then into manhood, handsome, strong,
My love for him, went on and on.
When trouble came, he'd always see,
How true a friend he had in me.

Those private things, he'd tell no other,
Confide and trust them to his mother.
For years, a source of pride and joy,
That was my Son,
My darling boy.

Then with no warning,
No, not one,
God took away my precious son.
Now memories cannot replace
The presence of that lovely face.
Nor can they touch, nor smile, nor start
To fill this hole left in my heart.

But memories are all I have,
Of you, my son, my big fine lad.
You've gone ahead, to pave the way,
For us to meet again, someday.

And when my time on earth is done,
I'll meet you once again,
My Son.

IRENE JACKSON

Look Forward to the Future

Look forward to the future, it has a rosy glow,
Relax and it will come to you just as the rivers flow.
Bubbling and laughing the river travels on,
Over rough and stony ground it sings its merry song.

Flowing gently sometimes beside the pastures green,
Then rushing in a torrent and racing down the stream;
Gliding on her surface comes the graceful swan
In all her snowy splendour, majestic in the sun.

The river is so full of life of creatures great and small,
It brings peace and tranquillity and hope to us all.
As the river keeps on flowing, it heads out to the sea
To join a greater life force just like you and me.

Look forward to the future and go with the flow.
Even though you worry that your progress may be slow:
For surely as the river flows out to the sea,
We are all travelling onwards to meet our destiny.

EILEEN COLEMAN

Mother, Oh Mother

Mother, Oh Mother, I miss you so much
Your warmth and your comfort your gentle touch.
It was you who held me in the darkness of night
When bad dreams awoke me and gave me a fright.

You were always there too when in illness or pain,
Your arms twined about me, crooning loves sweet refrain.
It was you, darling mother, who taught me to write
My very own words, all joined up just right.

You always encouraged me to give of my best,
To strive for perfection with good humour and zest;
And when I had fallen or things had gone wrong
You were always there, mother, with arms that were strong,

You'd wipe away my tears, gently stroke my brow,
Then cuddle and kiss me, showing me how
To pick up the pieces and begin again,
Trying even harder my goals to attain.

For if something's worth doing, it's worth doing well.
It raises the spirit in which we all dwell,
And I know one day, mother, we will both meet again
In a far lovelier place where there is no pain.

Where love and beauty so overwhelmingly preside
And where after long last. I'll be there by your side.

EILEEN COLEMAN

Did I Imagine?

Is it them or is it me?
Did I imagine or did I see?
Was that a tingle on my brow
From those in spirit or the here and now?

Was that an eagle in the sky
Or just the formation of clouds going by?
Was that really a guide smiling at me
or did I imagine what I hoped I'd see?

Oh dear Lord, I want to learn.
Please, Oh when will it be my turn?
I've been so patient and of late
I've felt there wasn't long to wait.

But just when I think I'm almost there,
The vision fades from my searching stare.
Please give me the wisdom to understand
Those who are helping in the Summerland.

They must be just as frustrated as me,
Waiting and longing for me to break free,
To shed my troubles, worries and strife,
And reach through the barrier that keeps us from life.

For it is not death that keeps us apart,
Only the worries that weigh down a heart,
And I know when I learn to communicate
There will be such joy at those golden gates.

My friends and my family will all rejoice
That at last I've found my spiritual voice.

EILEEN COLEMAN

Acknowledgements

The author wishes to express his thanks for permission to use copyright material to *Terence Carter* for the cartoon on page 31, the *Grantham Journal* for Messages From The Grave on page 75, *Jim Carter* for the photograph of Sam Tomlinson on page 93, the *Boston and Sleaford Standard* for Happy Medium on page 96 and the *Sleaford Standard* for Spirit Led Me on page 109.

By the Same Author

Just a Touch Away
I'm Here Listening
Spirit, My Second Home